Crime and the Elderly

Crime and
the Elderly

Challenge and Response

Edited by
Jack Goldsmith
The American University

Sharon S. Goldsmith
The American University

Lexington Books
D.C. Heath and Company
Lexington, Massachusetts
Toronto

Library of Congress Cataloging in Publication Data

National Conference on Crime Against the Elderly, Washington, D.C., 1975.
    Crime and the elderly.

    Includes bibliographical references and index.
    1. Aged—United States—Crimes against—Congresses. I. Goldsmith, Jack. II. Goldsmith, Sharon S. III. Title.
HV6250.4.A34N37   1975   364   75-42932
ISBN 0-669-00561-4

Published simultaneously in Canada.

Printed in the United States of America.

International Standard Book Number: 0-669-00561-4

Library of Congress Catalog Card Number: 75-42932

Contents

Preface

The National Conference on Crime Against the Elderly was held June 5-7, 1975, in Washington, D.C., by The American University College of Public Affairs under a grant from the Administration on Aging, U.S. Department of Health, Education and Welfare. The conference was the first national forum to address the problem of the criminal victimization of older persons. The purpose of the conference was to bring together concerned practitioners and scholars in the areas of aging services and criminal justice to share information and discuss the problem of crime against the aging and approaches to reduce the criminal victimization of the aging.

This book contains selected papers presented at the conference. The authors are distinguished scholars and practitioners whose early recognition of the problem of crime against the elderly and work in this important area provides the best available base for future research and program development. The selections illustrate several dimensions of the problem—patterns of victimization, the plight of the older victim, and the response to the problem. Although the various authors have differing approaches and major concerns, the underlying theme is that crime and the fear of crime dramatically and often tragically affect the quality of life for millions of older Americans. It is hoped that the conference and this book will serve to encourage research and action to reduce the burden of crime on older Americans.

The editors wish to thank each author for contributing to this book as well as the other participants in the National Conference on Crime Against the Elderly for their innovative and very significant work in the area of crime and the elderly. In addition, appreciation for support and encouragement must go to Arthur S. Flemming, United States commissioner on aging, and Morris W.H. Collins, dean, College of Public Affairs, The American University.

1 Crime and the Elderly: An Overview

Jack Goldsmith and
Sharon S. Goldsmith

Crime is one of the greatest problems in America today. It is one of the principal considerations that occupies our thoughts and shapes the way we live. In spite of the increasing number of anticrime programs, rates of reported crimes grow steadily each year. Recent victimization surveys that project actual (as opposed to reported) crime rates indicate there are two or three times more crimes committed than reported to authorities. Public opinion surveys repeatedly cite crime—along with the economy—at or very near the top of public concerns.

Victims of crime come in all ages, colors, and social classes, and criminals are not respectors of ability to recover from loss or ability to protect oneself. For many categories of crime recognized by criminal justice authorities as "serious," data indicate that older people may be less likely to be victimized than the general population. Although crime data that include the age of the victim are sparse, and thus conclusions are tentative on this point, it has long been assumed that older people are less victimized, that the types of crimes committed against them are not as "serious," and therefore that criminal victimization of older persons quite rightly should not receive priority in the criminal justice system. These assumptions ignore the fact that reliance on raw crime statistics oversimplifies the crime problem and does not allow for analysis of qualitative aspects of crime. Until recently such a reliance on statistics was the dominant approach within the law enforcement community: singling out victims according to age, therefore, was rarely done. However, this traditional approach is changing.

Perspectives on older people and how they fit into American society is also undergoing revision. There is a growing awareness in the general population and heightened consciousness among older people themselves regarding the problems, needs, and rights of older Americans. There is increasing recognition that in many ways older people are an oppressed—and growing—minority for whom "senior citizenship" has often meant second-class citizenship. As the aging segment of the population increases and as political and governmental leaders have recognized the need for special programs, older persons and their advocates in and out of government have begun to organize to promote improvements in the programs that affect the quality of life.

Public policy affecting the elderly in areas such as income, transportation, housing, and health care has been targeted to respond to the particular needs of the elderly. There is now a movement to approach the problem of crime and the elderly in such terms. This changing conceptualization of the criminal victimiza-

1

tion of the elderly and of the response to it is based on consideration of the problem on its own terms rather than as a part of the general crime configuration as depicted in aggregate, nonage-based crime statistics.

We know, for instance, that although older people are the victims of the same kinds of crime as the general population, they are "undervictimized" in certain categories (murder) and "overvictimized" in others (fraud, personal larceny.) Analysis of patterns of crimes committed against older persons suggest the need for a specialized index of crimes against the elderly. Such an index might, for example, focus attention on crimes such as purse snatching, medical fraud, con games and schemes, pension frauds, assault, retirement and land sale frauds, burglary, vandalism, and abuse or neglect in nursing homes. There are important reasons for the development of this approach to the problem of crime and the elderly.

One major reason for focusing special attention on crime against the elderly is the differential impact of crime and increased vulnerability of the elderly. There are physical, economic, and environmental factors associated with aging that increase vulnerability to criminal attack and that magnify the impact of victimization. Aging is a period of decreasing physical strength and agility making resistance to attack both less effective and more dangerous than for younger persons. Even relatively minor injuries may result in serious and perhaps permanent damage to the older victim. The prospect of severe and lasting disability from a brief encounter with a purse snatcher is particularly frightening for an older person.

Old age is also a time of diminished income and fewer economic resources. Dependence on small, fixed incomes from social security or other retirement payments and perhaps some limited savings often make old age a period of economic insecurity. The loss of a relatively few dollars—although it might be classified by authorities as a petty crime—can have a very dramatic or tragic effect on the life of an older person who is without financial resources to replace money needed for food, medicine, rent, and other necessities.

Increased vulnerability and differential impact are also related to environmental and social factors associated with being old in America. It is often necessary for older persons to live in or near high crime areas of cities. Reasonably priced housing for single persons is often not available in more secure, suburban neighborhoods. Greater reliance on public transportation or on walking can also increase exposure to criminal attack.

It is not only purse snatchers who seek out older victims; "white-collar criminals" and con men prey on older persons. The social situation of the newly retired or widowed person can enhance vulnerability to a wide variety of schemes that appear to insure financial gain, lifetime security, or relief from physical suffering or loneliness. The list of frauds perpetrated against and designed for the elderly is a long one. For the perpetrator of fraud and bunco—as for the robber or burglar—the vulnerability of the older person serves as a green light.

Due in part to their special vulnerability and the differential impact of crime, fear of criminal victimization can be particularly pervasive among older persons. The "crime problem" has two aspects—the actual threat of victimization and the perceived threat. Fear is a product of the perceived threat. In many cases the fear of crime may be unwarranted when considered in relation to actual crime rates: this is particularly the case regarding violent crime—fear of assault, rape, mugging, and murder may be extreme.

The fearful environment that people of all ages experience in urban and suburban America can be particularly threatening to an older person. Awareness of one's own limitations and vulnerabilities quite understandably can cause an exaggerated sense of helplessness and fearfulness. One response to a fearful environment is to withdraw from community life in order to remain "secure" behind locked doors. Although this response may or may not be a rational adaptation in a given situation, the result is still a diminution of personal freedom and an assault on the quality of life available to the individual.

Victims have not been an overriding concern for law enforcement and the other parts of the criminal justice system. The "function" of the victim was to initiate a complaint, to provide information to aid in the investigation, and finally to serve as a prosecution witness. Over the years, a law enforcement response paradigm developed that focused attention and concern on the criminal act and the offender—not on the victim. Since victims were not major components of this equation, the response to crime against an older person was essentially the same as the response to crime against a person of any age. Under this response paradigm, there was no special recognition given to the differential impact of crime on certain groups of victims.

This traditional response to crime grew in part out of a desire to provide equal treatment to avoid both favoritism and prejudicial treatment by law enforcement. The ideal of equal treatment, however, does not take into consideration any special requirements or characteristics of victims. Although special treatment for children who are crime victims—as well as offenders—is long recognized in law, other groups of victims (such as the elderly and rape victims) are only now demanding and receiving specialized treatment from criminal justice agencies.

The present thrust in criminal justice practice builds on the traditional crime and criminal-centered concerns, yet goes well beyond to include a victim orientation, and, further, recognizes the role of the community in crime control. A growing victim orientation has characterized criminal justice policy in the past few years. The rise of the field of victimology, presidential statements on crime that stress the plight of victims, and the expansion of rape victim and battered child programs have paved the way for specialized programs to reduce crime against the elderly and to assist the older victim of crime.

An important component of the new victim consciousness is the victim advocate concept. Police departments, prosecutors' offices, and other agencies are experimenting with victim advocate programs. In some cases, a special unit or a single officer has a specific mission to deal with older victims. These programs may provide counselling, information and referral to emergency services, advice and assistance in preparing for court appearances, and instruction in crime prevention. The criminal justice community is becoming increasingly aware that crime control is a goal that requires broad community support and cooperation. Community-based crime control programs—many established specifically for older people—are becoming widespread. Target-hardening (personal and residential security) seminars at senior centers and clubs are being established throughout the country. The roster of crime-prevention and victim-assistance programs for the elderly is growing and represents a great variety of activity by both public and private sectors to reduce the burden of crime against the elderly.

Bibliography

A Symposium on Crime and the Elderly, *The Police Chief* (February 1976).

Report and papers from the National Conference on Crime Against the Elderly (College of Public Affairs, The American University, Washington, D.C., 1975).

Goldsmith, Jack. Community Crime Prevention and the Elderly: A Segmental Approach. *Crime Prevention Review*, Vol. 2, No. 4, July 1975.

Goldsmith, Jack, and Noel E. Tomas. Crimes Against the Elderly: A Continuing National Crisis. *Aging* June-July 1974.

Goldsmith, Sharon S., and Jack Goldsmith. Crime, the Aging and Public Policy. *Perspective on Aging* May-June 1975.

**Part I
Patterns of Crime Against
the Elderly**

2

Defrauding the Elderly

Gilbert Geis

Frauds against the elderly appear to differ notably from crimes of violence in regard to some of the characteristics of the victims. The brunt of violent crime directed at old persons clearly falls disproportionately upon the poor and the inner-city aged.[a] Large-scale frauds, however, tend to be perpetrated against more affluent and well-to-do elderly victims. As Herbert Edelhertz, formerly chief of the Fraud Section of the Criminal Division of the federal Department of Justice, has noted:

The very poor, and particularly the destitute elderly, are not profitable targets for those engaged in white-collar criminal activities. They may "pay more,"[b] as some surveys have indicated, but they are relatively impervious to the general harassment of process servers and collection agents, whose success is the ultimate reliance and *raison d'etre* of every consumer fraud operation. If a mother on welfare is given a short weight when she buys food, the impact on her family is clear, but the transaction itself is not a vehicle for continued oppression and victimization.[1]

Edelhertz' statement rather misses the point, however, for it requires very little further deprivation for many of the elderly poor to reduce them to utter misery, or death, and it is not the relative amount of exploitation, but its particularly heinous nature that is important in regard to older persons.[2]

Indeed, whether directed against the well-to-do or the impoverished, fraud stands as a highly reprehensible criminal act, and it is a form of criminal behavior that for too long has gone underattended and underpunished in the United States. This relative indifference is a heritage of early laissez-faire attitudes that regarded with condescension the exploitation of the weak by the unscrupulous. The thirteenth century English courts, Frederick Pollock and F.W. Maitland

---

[a]It is often pointed out, however, that as a group the elderly are much less often victims of street crimes than young persons. The recent crime victimization survey conducted under the auspices of the federal Bureau of the Census in eight so-called "impact cities" found that "personal victimization peaks in the 16-19 age groups and declines monotonically beyond that point." The rate of assaultive violence without theft for those in the 16-19-year-old group was 76 per 1,000, and the rate in the 65 and older group was only 6 per 1,000. See Michael J. Hindelang, *An Analysis of Victimization Survey Results from the Eight Impact Cities: Summary Report* (Latham, N.Y.: Criminal Justice Research Center, 1974), pp. 18-20. See also Jaber F. Gubrium, "Victimization in Old Age: Available Evidence and Three Hypotheses," *Crime and Delinquency*, 20 (July 1974), pp. 245-250.

[b]The reference is to David Caplovitz, *The Poor Pay More: Consumer Practices of Low-Income Families* (New York: The Free Press, 1963).

7

observed, "had no remedy for the man who to his damage had trusted the word of a liar."[3] Even in the eighteenth century, a British chief justice could rhetorically ask: "When A got money from B by pretending that C had sent for it, shall we indict one man for making a fool of another?"[4] It was only in 1757 that a statutory provision for the punishment of "mere private cheating" was placed into English law.[5]

Nonetheless, it was about 250 years ago, in 1726, that the English essayist, Jonathan Swift, a biting critic of injustice, passed a definitive judgment on fraud. The Lilliputians, Swift observed in *Gulliver's Travels*, "look upon fraud as a greater crime than theft . . . for they allege that care and vigilance, with a very common understanding, may preserve a man's goods from thieves, but honesty has no defense against superior cunning."[6] Swift had his fictive Lilliputians decree death as the only suitable response to so abhorrent and intolerable a behavior as fraud.

Capital punishment may be too harsh a response to fraud today, although there are individual cases that might persuade even intense antagonists of the death penalty otherwise. But certain legislative reforms are essential. The elderly are particularly vulnerable to fraud, and they have earned the right to special protection just as such protection has been afforded to infants and young persons.

In particular, frauds whose victims are located among the elderly ought to be singled out for much more severe penalties than they currently carry. This would include the various forms of medical and nursing home deceits that prey upon elderly persons as well as acts such as the pigeon drop confidence game.[7] A story in the *Denver Post* is characteristic of similar accounts that appear regularly in newspapers. The *Denver Post* reported the case of Mrs. Sarah Griggs, 72, who lost her savings of 19 years, $2,500, to two women using the pigeon drop scheme.[c]

There is at the moment some nascent precedence for the proposed imposition of heavier penalties upon criminals who prey upon the elderly. In California, state Senator George Deukmejian introduced during the 1975-76 session of the legislature a measure calling for a period of imprisonment of not less than two or more than five years, above the regular sentence, for persons who commit or attempt to commit a crime of bodily injury against an individual who is 65 years or older, or who is blind, paraplegic, or quadraplegic.[d]

Thus, just as some Oriental legal systems decree that matricide and parricide are particularly heinous crimes carrying heavier penalties than other murders,[8]

---

[c]*Denver Post*, September 14, 1974. The name and address of the victim have been changed. In a letter to the *New York Times* (August 30, 1954), Michael Walpin commented on a news report about a 75-year-old nurse being robbed of $6,000 in a pigeon-drop ruse by suggesting that bank officials be more careful in allowing withdrawals by older persons and that they propose the money be taken in a cashier's check rather than in cash.

[d]Senate Bill No. 615. The measure passed the Senate by a large majority and was awaiting hearing by the Assembly Committee on Criminal Justice at the end of the summer of 1975.

so too might we testify to our concern for the elderly by establishing better safeguards for them. But the protection afforded by more stringent sentences ought to be extended beyond bodily injury offenses to cover crimes of fraud. Such statutes would not be in violation of equal protection standards of the Constitution, but rather would serve to provide more equal protection than now exists.[e]

The evidence seems reasonably clear that fraud and property deprivation are behaviors that are particularly susceptible to deterrence through suitable enforcement practices and penalty structures.[9] These are offenses that are more likely than crimes of violence to be impelled by considered self-interest and rational predatory judgment. One is reminded of W.C. Fields, playing a small town thief about to rob a sleeping cowboy. He changed his mind, however, when he discovered that the cowboy was wearing a revolver. "It would be dishonest," he remarked virtuously as he tiptoed away.[10]

The rationale for the belief that harsher penalties and more vigorous enforcement would provide much better protection for the elderly lies in the fact that so-called "white-collar criminals"[11] are apt to find tangling with the criminal justice system highly unnerving.[f] Conversely, as George Jackson noted, "Black men born in the U.S. and fortunate enough to live past the age of eighteen are conditioned to accept the inevitability of prison."[12] Statements suggesting the efficacy of criminal justice sanctions against persons perpetrating fraud are commonplace. An early thesis is that of Edward A. Ross, who believed that the "brake of prison walls" represented the best approach to controlling criminal business and professional men—the "slippery wheels" of society.[13]

Further justification for tougher responses to crimes against the elderly may be found in the fact that the social consequences of such behavior may well be more deleterious than those resulting from more traditional kinds of offenses. Emile Durkheim, a French sociologist, has argued convincingly that traditional crime tends to cement a society by providing object lessons to the well-behaved about the consequences of aberrance.[14] Fraud, on the other hand, is said to rend severely the social fabric by creating distrust and encouraging rationalizations for deviance. On this point, the report of the President's Commission on

---

[e]Some persons, indeed, might find it odd that the proposed revision of the Criminal Code of the United States notes that "(w)hether the offender is elderly or in poor health" is a matter that ought to be taken into account in determining his sentence, but that there is no mention of the age or state of health of the victim as a matter of any importance. National Commission on Reform of Federal Criminal Laws, *Study Draft of a New Federal Criminal Code* (Washington, D.C.: U.S. Government Printing Office, 1970), § 3101(3) (1).

[f]Senator Phillip Hart made the point well: "One businessman—or politician—can watch another get fired without feeling serious psychological discomfort. But to see your counterpart from across town or across the aisle marched away in blue denims with black stenciling is highly unnerving. . . . On the other hand, the threat of the same jail term would likely be wasted on an unemployed ghetto youth with an impulse to burglarize a record shop. So why not allocate some of our prison space where it would do the most good?" Hart, "Swindling and Knavery, Inc.," *Playboy* (August 1972), p. 158.

Law Enforcement and Administration of Justice maintained that "white-collar crime affects the whole moral climate of our society."[15]

Russell Baker put the matter with bittersweet facetiousness in a recent article he called, "The Old Rush." "I don't know why old people ought to be an exploitable business commodity, but the lessons of the nursing home scandals[16] is that they are," Baker wrote. "I think there ought to be an age at which everybody draws the line—maybe 70 or 75—and says, 'All right, your reward for making it this far is that nobody can make a profit on you.'" Baker noted that he did not look forward to serving in his later years as a Klondike for entrepreneurs working the old-people business: ". . . I want to be able to walk on the beach and watch the sun go down without having some guy in an expensive suit nagging me to come back and turn him some profit before it gets dark."[17]

The Exposed Position of the Elderly

Very little study has gone into the subject of crime victimization,[g] and even less, inevitably, into the particular assailability of the aged. The classic statement remains that of Hans von Hentig, whose *The Criminal and His Victim* (1948) devotes 379 pages to the first part of its title and only 70 pages to the second. Significantly, the heading of von Hentig's discourse on crime victims is called "Victim's Contribution to the Genesis of Crime," a theme that accords with the continuing obsession on the part of students of crime victimization with demonstrating that in some manner the object of a criminal depradation "asked for" what he or she got.[h]

Such aberrant excursions aside, von Hentig concentrates on matters that remain important today. In particular, he notes that insufficient attention has been paid to the death of "old and decrepit people hospitalized in private homes and the large number of deaths by fire." In regard to both of these, von Hentig makes the following observations:

In the first case the situation presents an incentive to get rid of the old patient, since a lump sum is paid so that the old man be cared for for the "rest of his

---

[g]There has, however, been a recent surge in interest in crime victims. Attention to the subject began with the victimization surveys conducted by the President's Commission on Law Enforcement and Administration of Justice. For a general overview see Israel Drapkin and Emilio Viano, eds., *Victimology* (Lexington, Mass.: Lexington Books, D.C. Heath, 1974).

[h]See, for example, Menachim Amir, "Victim Precipitated Forcible Rape," *Journal of Criminal Law, Criminology and Police Science*, 58 (December 1967), pp. 493-502. For a critique of Amir's position see Kurt Weis and Sandra S. Borges, "Victimology and Rape: The Case of the Legitimate Victim," *Issues in Criminology*, 8 (Fall 1973), pp. 71-115. Wolfgang's work, demonstrating that many victims of homicide are themselves aggressive persons, with criminal records for violent acts, stands as an exception to this criticism. (Cf., Marvin E. Wolfgang, *Patterns in Criminal Homicide* [Philadelphia: University of Pennsylvania Press, 1958]).

life." The danger lies in the fluidity of this period; a reduction of the interval promises profit and infirmity renders the diagnosis of cause of death difficult. As to the second category, approximately 15,000 deaths are caused by fire every year in the United States. . . . Too many people . . . are burned by exploding oil burners, or while burning weeds or leaves in the barnyard, or are said to have fallen asleep while smoking and thus ignited their bedding. . . . In all such fires babies and old people are the main sufferers.[18]

At least one remedy is implicit in von Hentig's material. It would involve the outlawing of lump-sum payments to nursing homes by the elderly who enter such facilities and the establishment of state-operated or private trust funds that would handle financial arrangements with the homes.

That von Hentig's insights of more than a quarter of a century ago are relevant today is shown in the remarks of Robert Leonard, a prosecuting attorney in Michigan, before the Senate Committee on the Judiciary last year. Leonard discussed mobile homes, which, because of financial necessity, are disproportionately the housing of the elderly:

Another area which has been of extreme concern to my office . . . is the mobile home industry. Many Americans . . . have been required to accept fire and safety hazards which are inherent in the numerous, presently mass-produced mobile homes which . . . are being manufactured under the most minimally protective "industry" codes and regulations which can be imagined.

In [my county] alone in the last few months at least 10 persons have died horrible and agonizing deaths in at least 22 mobile home fires. There have also been many other such fires and similar deaths across the state of Michigan in the same time period. . . .[19]

Leonard argued that a "pro-industry" bias existing at the state level in Michigan had operated to deny all efforts to have consumer interests fairly and impartially considered in regard to the issue of mobile home safety.[20]

My own introduction to the poignancy and the vulnerability of the position of the elderly came early in my academic career when I undertook to study the work of Knut Hamsun, a Norwegian who was awarded the Nobel Prize in Literature in 1920.[21] Hamsun had what amounted to a pathological dread of old age. In *Benoni*, written in 1908, when Hamsun was 48-years old, he described two men in their dotage:

These two ancients, their faces smeared with grease, filthy about the hands, smelling of old age, disseminate a loathesomeness beyond measure over their end of the room, a feeling of bestiality which travels along the table on both sides.[22]

The fates were to have their ironic revenge, though, for Hamsun himself lived to be 92. When he was 80, the Germans invaded Norway, and Hamsun, in part prodded by his wife who formerly had been married to a German and had strong ties with that country, became a Nazi sympathizer. After the war, in his

90th year, Hamsun published *Paa Gjengrodde Stier*, a book attempting to defend against the charges of treachery, based on his visits with Hitler and Goebbels, and his published pro-Nazi statements. Hamsun tried to convey in his defense what it meant to be old and isolated:

No one told me it was wrong for me to keep writing; no one in the entire country. I sat alone in my room, shut off by myself. I did not hear, I was so deaf; no one had anything to do with me. They banged on a stovepipe for me from below when I should come and eat; that noise I heard. I went down, got my food and went up again by myself and sat. For months, for all these years it was like this. . . . And never did a small sign come to me . . . a little good advice from the surrounding world. No, the outside world keep itself aloof. And it seldom or never happened that I got a little information or any help from my household or family. I had to have everything in writing, and it got too tedious. I remained sitting there.[i]

Kinds of Cozenage

The blatant manipulation of elderly persons who often are in poignant and anguished quest for things denied them because of their years—things such as surcease from pain or loneliness, or alleviation of the fear of imminent death—makes fraud against them particularly ugly and despicable. There is also something sad in the idea, advanced by a California consumer affairs bureau director, that the "elderly are careless about making a purchase, perhaps because they're used to a time when people were more trustworthy."[j]

The forms of cozenage seem restricted only by the limits on the guile and duplicity of the perpetrators.[23] A grieving widow receives a Bible in the mail that allegedly had been ordered by her husband just before his death. There is a bill for $50, although the item truly is worth no more than one-tenth that amount.[24] Six million persons in the United States who suffer from arthritis— almost half of those stricken with the disease and most of them elderly persons—are gulled into spending almost a quarter of a million dollars each year on quack, worthless remedies.[k] In this regard, Dr. L.F. Saylor, the former

[i]Knut Hamsun, *Paa Gjengrodde Stier* (Oslo: Gyldendal, 1949), pp. 150-151. The translation is mine. An English language version is Hamsun, *On Overgrown Paths*, trans. by Carl L. Anderson (New York: Eriksson, 1967), with the cited passage on p. 142.

[j]Jim Shimanoff, quoted in Steve Kline, "Consumers' Don Quizote Jousts with Hustlers," *Los Angeles Times* (Orange County edition), August 22, 1973. The same official has a sign on his wall reading: "Populus Lambudum Defutatus Est," which, loosely translated, means: "The public has been screwed long enough."

[k]"What the Health Hucksters Are Up To," *Changing Times*, the *Kiplinger Magazine* (September 1964), pp. 24-29. See further James H. Young, *The Medical Messiahs* (Princeton, N.J.:Princeton University Press, 1967). The roots of susceptibility to such fraud are examined in Viola W. Bernard, "Why People Become the Victims of Medical Quackery," *American Journal of Public Health*, 55 (August 1965), pp. 1142-1147.

director of the California Department of Public Health, has noted that "(q)uackery kills more people than all the crimes of violence put together."[25]

Then there are the con artists who, in their inelegant but instructive terminology, "pencil-whip the mark" by promising a combination of home improvements and debt consolidation, all to be accompanied by lower monthly payments than are now being made. Figures are scrawled helter-skelter on a pad to demonstrate this illusory outcome. When the contract is signed, the fleecer turns the paper over to a finance company,[26] and sets forth after another—again to employ the con artists's terminology—"mom" or "lamb."[27]

The roster of case histories of frauds against the elderly is virtually endless. There was the 78-year old woman, confined totally to a wheelchair, who was sold a 175-week exercise program by a high-pressure talker from a major national health spa.[28] There are similar schemes involving phony contests, securities and commodity frauds, merchandise swindles, bait advertising, charitable solicitation frauds, funeral service contracts, credit manipulations, and multitudinous other deceptions.[1]

Perhaps the most telling manner of conveying the nature of such episodes is not by detailing their ingredients but by presenting the views of the victims, a large portion of them elderly persons, in their own words, as they express their feelings. To accomplish this, I use quotations from letters—in all there were more than 30,000—sent to the special assistant for the president for Consumer Affairs, extracts of which came my way when I was working for the President's Commission on Law Enforcement. The special assistant's summary of these letters is itself worth noting:

The most striking feature, in our opinion, is not the allegations of criminal fraud that occasionally have been made to us by the correspondents. Rather, it is the sense of unfairness, of disregard of the individual by the organized business community, of lack of effective recourse, and of a feeling that the marketplace is unethical.[29]

These are some excerpts from the letters, with the emphases added:

I am a woman living alone on pension and have to be economical. I think it a shame that we have to consistently *fight to survive*.

I bought a cotton suit at Vieboldt's Store, washed it by hand and it streaked, faded and dripped. $12 is not a small sum. The Vieboldt's people told me I was to expect cotton to run and shrink. *The idea that they think they can get away with this kind of thing makes me very mad.*

I find instead of winning anything, I have entered into a fictitious prize contract.

---

[1]For a detailed report on such matters see U.S. Senate, Special Committee on Aging, Subcommittee on Frauds and Misrepresentation Affecting the Elderly, *Report*, 89th Cong., 1st Sess., 1965.

I am being hounded, harassed, threatened, and the privacy of my home is being invaded. I will continue to withhold payment under such threats.

I have just finished wasting one hour with a young man representing Crowell-Collier Encyclopedia. His pitch I am embarrassed to admit—that he was merely doing an advertising survey; that he wished to place 30 encyclopedias in 30 homes, free. At the end, of course, comes the nice ploy that one must, in return, buy a supplement set for $37.50 per year for 10 years. *The lack of morality, the blatant lie, the spinning of the web of deception* in the minds of those of us who are professionally concerned with integrity. . . .

I have become a victim of otosclorosis and I am becoming gradually deaf. I have paid $625 for two hearing aids and pay $0.25 for each battery. This has been a very difficult thing to endure because I am sure that they cost very little to manufacture. I have endured the cost of these things with great difficulties. *The sellers of these aids make me positively ill.*

We retired people in moderate financial circumstances are *becoming aggravated to the extent that we must appeal to the Federal Government.*

The Elderly Crime Victim in Court

There is another area that notably bears on the problems of the elderly in their dealings with the criminal justice system as victims of fraud. That concerns the reactions of the authorities once they have been made aware of the criminal behavior. The elderly often do not make good witnesses: they can be easily flustered by a relentless defense attorney,[30] their memories may be on the vague side when precise details are demanded, and they are not readily able to get to court promptly since they often do not have adequate transportation.

Interviews that I conducted in California with persons receiving assistance from the crime victim compensation program—a considerable portion of whom were elderly individuals—bear out the callous indifference that the system demonstrates toward those whom it is particularly charged with assisting.[31]

Two particular conclusions emerged from that study of crime victims:

First, it is fortunate for the functionaries in the adjudication stage in the criminal justice system that they have a monopoly on the administration of justice. Rarely has a group been so uniformly regarded with so little respect, much less admiration, by those with whom they do business. That there are important consequences of this low esteem seems undeniable: it is reflected in crime reporting rates, in local and national elections, and in similar significant ways.

Second, it is fortunate for the same functionaries that those who they offend tend to be among the most powerless persons within our society. Insulated on high, judges are grandly protected from the disparagement that was so routinely divulged to us by the crime victims whose cases the courts had handled. Abraham Blumberg has nicely portrayed the in-group camaraderie and clubbiness that marks the performance of officials in the criminal justice system.[32] In their private lives, the officials generally mingle to a large extent with persons who never have reason to experience the indifference that the elderly, the poor, and the others who constitute the corps of crime victims maintain that they receive.

Many victims feel their needs have extremely low priority and that, at best, they are tolerated and then often with ill humor. Their role, they say, seems much like that of the expectant father in the hospital at delivery time: necessary for things to have gotten underway in the past but at the moment rather superfluous and mildly bothersome. Victims will sometimes note that the offenders seem to fare a good deal better than they do: the offender, at least, is regarded by criminal justice functionaries as a doer, an antagonist, someone to be wary of, a person who must be manipulated successfully if the workers in the system—the police, the judge, the attorneys—are to have their rewards for a job well done. The victim, on the other hand, is part of the background scenery—a rather drab character, in the nature of a spear-carrying supernumerary, watching from a distance the preening and posturing of the prima donna stars in the drama.

The following are but two of the remedial steps that ought to be taken:

1. Someone has to be designated to see that victims get a fairer shake if only in the name of public relations. A letter informing them of the disposition of their case, thanking them for their cooperation, explaining to them what will go on or what has gone on would be a minimum fulfillment of the dictates of courtesy.

2. Someone has to attend to scheduling that takes into account inconveniences to the victims and see to it that adequate compensation is afforded for the time spent in court appearances. As Edelhertz has noted:

. . . the total impact on victims in a consumer fraud case could be staggering and, in a sense, add insult to injury. Everyone involved in grand jury investigations can tell stories of groups of victims and witnesses subpoened to testify, asked to come back time after time because they were not reached on the initial subpoena date, and these impositions are aggravated by delays and continuances after indictment and trial stages.[33]

3. Systems of crime victim compensation[34] that include not only medical and loss-of-earning reparations, but also social service assistance—not as charity, but as the right of a citizen in need—should be mounted and expanded. For the elderly, such programs ought to go beyond the usual restrictions that compensation will only cover injuries from crimes of violence. Every loss to the elderly traceable to victimization that is not repaired from other sources ought to be remedied as best as possible by victim compensation efforts.

Conclusion

The jargon of the social scientist would have it that there is a special "eliciting sociocultural matrix" that makes the elderly particularly susceptible to victimization by fraud. About 13 years ago, in our criminology textbook, Herbert A. Bloch and I sought to indicate, by reference to the elderly, how crimes reflect and are responsive to social conditions and cultural organization at a particular period in history. We illustrated that mouthful of theoretical superstructure by describing the operation of certain confidence games that are distinctive for the United States. In one such operation, we noted, a seemingly affluent man, posing as an investment counselor, preys upon large drifting populations of widows in the playgrounds of the aged, Florida and southern California. The special sociocultural elements that enable such an operation to flourish are the greater longevity of women compared to men; the life insurance benefits that accrue to widows; the enormous increase in per capita income in the United States during the past half-century that has encouraged mobility and the establishment of large semitropical areas of retirement and relaxation. Also important was the fact that for most married women today parental responsibility ends in the early 40s. Thus, the cultural system produces a special group of persons who become vulnerable to victimization and a special set of circumstances that render their exploitation feasible.[35]

Such theoretical musings do not, however, allow us to proceed very far beyond the observation that in the final analysis it is the culture itself in the United States that bears most fundamentally the "responsibility" for the criminal victimization by any of us or of any of us—be we young, middle-aged, or elderly.

Note might be made, in this regard, of the estimate that in the United States, in large part because of the private practice of medicine, there are probably 10,000 or more deaths that occur from what is estimated to be more than 2 million unnecessary operations, many of them frauds against the elderly.[36] When the Mine Worker's Fund, concerned with what it believed were unnecessary operations, added the requirement that all such work be endorsed by a preoperative specialist, the number of operations fell by 75 percent for hysterectomies and 60 percent for appendectomies. It is believed that surgical fees lay at the heart of the matter: when doctors receive set salaries they operate less; when they get fees, they operate more—and more patients die.[37]

Changes in the values and ethos of our system that carry with them significant alterations in patterns of exploitation and fraud do not seem to be on the horizon. For the elderly, about all that can be assured is that their numbers will grow precipitously. It has been calculated that by the year 2000 1 in 5 persons will be over 65, compared with 1 in 10 today and 1 in 25 in 1900.[m]

m"New Outlook for the Aged," *Time*, June 2, 1975, pp. 44-45. A futurist has observed that "one might expect an increase with aging population of crimes which are predatory on that age group: various kinds of bilking schemes, crimes associated with insurance, estates, and manipulations of assets." Joseph F. Coates, "The Future of Crime in the United States from Now to the Year 2000," *Policy Sciences*, 3 (1972), p. 31.

It will be a mighty flock of "lambs" for the sharpsters to fleece.

In Biblical history the lamb, of course, was the symbol of innocence, the creature most worthy of God's protection. Clichés about those who God best protects seem today particularly applicable to the elderly. Old persons will have to act like those Greek mouflon, the predecessors of today's sheep, who used their pointed, ferocious horns to insure their safety and that of their group. A model for such vigilance might be the Retired Professionals Action Group (RPAG), an arm of the Public Citizen force organized by Ralph Nader. RPAG members have investigated the hearing aid industry and developed a model bill for regulation of hearing aid dealers and salesmen. They have also turned their attention to the evaluation of pension funds in order to bring about long overdue reforms. In addition, nursing homes were monitored, and a comprehensive survey was conducted of all state nursing home licensing agencies to determine their composition and capabilities.[38] This kind of effort can produce results, for as Wayne Leys has noted: "our institutions are geared for well-organized complaint by people who have some bargaining power; they are not responsive to unlettered misery."[39]

In summary, let it be stressed that the elderly are a precious part of American society. They are particularly susceptible to exploitation; therefore, there is a special need that they be provided through the agency of new laws with statutory shields against depredations directed against them. Such shields, I think, should take the form of harsher penalties and more intensive enforcement against crimes that bear particularly on the elderly as well as on criminal events that have the elderly as victims.

If nothing else, self-interest ought to dictate support of such a program since the elderly, with their infirmities, vulnerabilities, and their right to surcease from victimization, are nothing but the precursors of each of us, ourself.

Notes

1. Herbert Edelhertz, *The Nature, Impact and Prosecution of White-Collar Crime* (Washington, D.C.: U.S. Government Printing Office, 1970), p. 9.

2. See generally Jack Goldsmith and Noel E. Tomas, "Crimes Against the Elderly: A Continuing National Crisis," *Aging* (June-July 1974), pp. 1-5, and Daniel Thurman, "Psychological Impact of Crime and Physical Insecurity on the Older Person," in Noel E. Tomas, ed., *Reducing Crimes Against Aged Persons*. Report of the Mid-Atlantic Federal Regional Council Task Force Workshop, January 1974, n.p.

3. Frederick Pollock and Frederic W. Maitland, *History of English Law* (Boston: Little, Brown, 1909), Vol. II, p. 535.

4. Quoted in Hermann Mannheim, *Criminal Justice and Social Reconstruction* (London: Routledge, 1946), p. 121.

5. *False Pretenses Act*, 30 George II, ch. 24.

18

6. Jonathan Swift, "A Voyage to Lilliput," in *Gulliver's Travels*, Part I, ch. 6.

7. See generally James T. Barbash, "Compensation and the Crime of Pigeon Dropping," *Journal of Clinical Psychology*, 8 (October 1951), pp. 92-94.

8. Melvin M. Belli and Danny R. Jones, *Belli Looks at Life and Law in Japan* (Indianapolis: Bobbs-Merrill, 1950), p. 129.

9. See Gilbert Geis, "Deterring Corporate Crime," in Ralph Nader and Mark J. Green, eds., *Corporate Power in America* (New York: Grossman, 1973), pp. 182-197; see generally Franklin E. Zimring and Gordon J. Hawkins, *Deterrence: The Legal Threat in Crime Control* (Chicago: University of Chicago Press, 1973).

10. Quoted in Brooks Atkinson, *Broadway* (New York: Macmillan, 1970), pp. 315-316.

11. See generally, Edwin H. Sutherland, *White Collar Crime* (New York: Dryden, 1949); Gilbert Geis, ed., *The White-Collar Criminal* (New York: Atherton, 1968).

12. George Jackson, *Soledad Brother* (New York: Bantam, 1970), p. 9.

13. Quoted in John Herling, *The Great Price Conspiracy* (Washington, D.C.: Robert B. Luce, 1962), p. 289.

14. Emile Durkheim, *The Rules of Sociological Method* (1895), trans. by Sarah A. Solovay and John H. Mueller (New York: Free Press, 1938).

15. President's Commission on Law Enforcement and Administration of Justice, *The Challenge of Crime in a Free Society* Washington, D.C.: U.S. Government Printing Office, 1967), p. 104.

16. See generally Clare Townsend, *Old Age: The Last Segregation* (New York: Grossman, 1971); Robert Stevens and Rosemary Stevens, *Welfare Medicine in America* (New York: Free Press, 1975), Mary A. Mendelson, *Tender Loving Greed* (New York: Random House, 1975).

17. Russell Baker, "The Old Rush," *New York Times Magazine*, March 9, 1975, p. 7.

18. Hans von Hentig, *The Criminal and His Victim* (New Haven, Conn.: Yale University Press, 1948), pp. 409-410.

19. U.S. Senate, Committee on the Judiciary, Subcommittee on Criminal Laws and Procedures, Reform of Federal Criminal Laws, 94th Congress., lst Sess., 1974, Pt. XI, p. 7870.

20. Ibid. See generally Center for Auto Safety, *Mobile Homes: The Low-Cost Housing Hoax* (New York: Grossman, 1975).

21. See generally Gilbert Geis, "Knut Hamsun, 1859-1952," *The Norseman* (London), 10 (May-June 1952), pp. 160-166.

22. Knut Hamsun, *Benoni*, trans. by Arthur G. Chater (New York: Knopf, 1925), p. 47.

23. See generally Michael T. Kaufman, "Elderly Warned of Con Games as Complaints Rise," *New York Times*, March 28, 1973.

24. "Senior Citizens Told of Fraud Schemes Aimed at Elderly," *Los Angeles Times*, September 22, 1968.

25. Quoted in George Getze, "Quackery Worse than Crime, Doctor Says," *Los Angeles Times*, September 4, 1970.

26. "Public Loses Millions in Mail Fraud Schemes," *Los Angeles Times* (UPI), March 21, 1968.

27. Kaufman, "Elderly Warned of Con Games," note 33.

28. Kline, "Consumers' Don Quixote Jousts with Hustlers," note 32.

29. Letter from Esther Peterson, March 25, 1966.

30. See, for instance, Lewis W. Lake, *How to Win Lawsuits Before Juries* (New York: Prentice-Hall, 1954), pp. 164-165.

31. See Gilbert Geis, "Victims of Crimes of Violence and the Criminal Justice System," in Duncan Chappell and John Monahan, eds., *Violence and Criminal Justice* (Lexington, Mass.: Lexington Books, D.C. Heath, 1975), pp. 61-74.

32. Abrahan S. Blumberg, *Criminal Justice* (Chicago: Quadrangle, 1967).

33. Edelhertz, *The Nature, Impact and Prosecution of White-Collar Crime*, note 3, pp. 32-33.

34. See generally Herbert Edelhertz and Gilbert Geis, *Public Compensation to Victims of Crime* (New York: Praeger, 1974).

35. Herbert A. Bloch and Gilbert Geis, *Man, Crime, and Society* (New York: Random House, 1962), p. 578.

36. Sidney Wolfe, quoted in "10,000 Surgery Deaths A Year Held Needless," *Los Angeles Times* (AP), December 17, 1971.

37. John P. Bunker, "Surgical Manpower in the United States and in England and Wales," *New England Journal of Medicine*, 282 (January 15, 1970), pp. 135-144; see also report of Dr. Robert S. Myers, quoted in John A. Osmundsen, "Survey Criticizes 50% of Surgery," *New York Times*, October 5, 1961.

38. *Public Citizen Report*, Number 2, 1972-73.

39. Wayne A.R. Leys, "Ethics in American Business and Government: The Confused Issues," *Annals of the American Academy of Political and Social Science*, 378 (July 1968), p. 39.

3 Psychological Aspects of Crime and Fear of Crime

M. Powell Lawton,
Lucille Nahemow,
Silvia Yaffe, and
Steven Feldman

The psychological aspects of crime victimization among older people must be understood within the context of their total biological, psychological, and social functioning. Although older people always are surprising us by their ability to cope with adversity, the fact remains that if one is over 65 in our society, there is a higher probability that one's effectiveness will be limited from each of these points of view. In spite of the fact that only about 14 percent of this population can be characterized as totally or partially disabled (Shanas 1971), 85 percent suffer from one or more chronic illnesses, each of which adds an increment to the effort required to perform ordinary tasks. Nearly half have some impairment of activity due to these conditions.

On the psychological level, both the general public and gerontologists have long overestimated the degree to which advancing age reduces the intellectual functioning of older people (Schaie 1974). More recently, better information has begun to appear to help us sort out areas in which decrements due to aging may be expected and those in which no systematic age decrements occur. There do appear to be age-related changes in vision, hearing, muscular strength and coordination, and the speed with which reactions to external events can occur. These changes conspire to reduce the information-processing efficiency of the older person, especially where he is required to react to a complex, unfamiliar, or fast-paced environmental situation (note that general intelligence, memory, and judgment are *not* included among the skills that tend to become impaired by age alone). Although the evidence is less clear regarding older people's emotional adjustment, we do note that conditions such as chronic brain disease, depression, alcoholism, and suicidal states increase with age, in frequent association with physical illness. Finally, there is some evidence to suggest that environmental pressure, particularly where quick decisions are required, increases the anxiety of older people disproportionately and thereby interferes with their ability to respond adaptively.

On the social level, limitations on the effectiveness of the older person are particularly obvious, beginning with economic deprivation. Forced retirement and fixed incomes, in spite of the aid of better and more inclusive social security benefits, limit the ability of older people to purchase the goods and services that allow stress to stay within adaptive limits. The results of these deprivations may be seen variously in poor housing situations, lack of adequate transportation, or nutrition problems. The social networks of many older people become restricted not only for economic reasons, but because of the pervading ageism of our

21

society, loss of mobility due to poor health, and loss of opportunities due to the death of spouse, relatives, and friends.

These losses in the biological, psychological, and social areas may be seen as representing the probability that an older person's competence in responding to even the normal pressures of living may be reduced in many areas. Although we have many public examples of older people who are highly effective, the proportion who suffer from none of these deprivations is very small indeed. The deprivations are cumulative and add up to what we might call heightened vulnerability to stress.

It is worth considering in greater detail the psychological interior of the older person. In general, research evidence shows few personality changes that can be ascribed to aging alone. This lack, however, makes the few documented differences show up with greater clarity. B.L. Neugarten and her associates at the University of Chicago (1964) defined a personality trait of *active mastery*, the extent to which the individual sees himself as capable of dealing with problems through his own initiative. The passive pole of this dimension describes the person who *responds* to problems, that is, one who accepts stresses and tries to adapt to them, rather than attempting to reconstruct the sources of stress themselves. Research has shown that middle-aged people are more likely to show active mastery than are older people (Neugarten and associates 1964). Active mastery is related to the locus of control concept (Rotter 1966). *Internal locus* of control refers to the view that the individual is in control of the extent to which the environment can provide satisfactions. *External locus of control*, conversely, is the attitude that one's satisfactions depend on fate, chance, or events outside the individual's control.

We can reason that the deprivations detailed above not only limit the effectiveness of the older person's behavior, but also that the recognition of this lessened effectiveness is fed back into the individual's conceptions of self and environment. He both *is* more vulnerable and *feels* more vulnerable.

This systematic change in self-concept may then proceed to "infect" new areas of the self-environment system. That is, even environmental situations that have not in fact proved stressful to the individual, or situations to which he has not been exposed, may become sources of perceived threat. How important is such a perceived threat, as contrasted to a real one? The best evidence on this score comes from research by K.K. Schooler (1975), who studied the residential moves of a large number of older people three years after an extensive interview. As might have been predicted from other research on the relocation of elderly people, declines in morale and even in functional health occurred among many people who had moved. In addition, if a person merely expected to move in 1969, his morale and health tended to be poorer in 1972, regardless of whether he actually moved during the three years. Finally, the combination of expecting to move and actually moving had more pronounced negative consequences than did either the threat or the move alone. Thus, there is good reason to think that feeling vulnerable and being vulnerable may be separately and cumulatively related to the general well-being of older people.

The applicability of this stress model to crime victimization of the elderly should be obvious. It is helpful to distinguish among the actual victimization, exposure to crime, and the perceived threat of crime, suggesting that each of these may decrease the breadth of an older person's behavior and lower his feeling of life satisfaction.

Age-specific victimization rates have been the subject of considerable study. The last word has not yet been said about the relative frequencies with which older people are the targets of particular crimes, although information from recent victimization surveys clearly helped us to sort out many relevant facts. On the basis of the victimization studies on hand now (United States Department of Justice 1974a; 1975), it seems that the rate among the elderly is as high or higher than among younger people for robbery with injury and for larceny with personal contact, but considerably lower for most other crimes.

Crime exposure is even less well understood. Since many older people live in poor urban neighborhoods with a high incidence of crime, it is not difficult to infer that such residents have a higher probability of being exposed than those living in middle class or less densely populated neighborhoods. In statistical terms, however, older residents would have the same exposure as younger residents of the same area. The critical consideration regarding comparative exposure rates is whether the behavioral patterns of young and old differ in ways that produce differential exposure within the same neighborhood. For the most part we have only armchair knowledge to guide us here. It is reasonable to think that older people leave their households less than younger people, considering their retirement status, lowered income, and health. We have also heard many anecdotal reports about specific measures taken by older people to lower their exposure, such as limiting the frequency, routes, destinations, or times of day when they leave their households. Unfortunately, there is a surprising lack of good information enabling us to state firmly what age-specific behavioral exposure rates might be. In some cases, such as S.M. Golant's (1972) study of Toronto, the number of trips by the elderly to nonwork destinations was surprisingly similar to those by people aged 55-64. (In this case one can suggest that the lack of age differences may partly reflect Toronto's low crime rate.) However, we badly need research to tell us how the well-known tendency of older people to stay home after dark compares with similar rates for other age groups; how much restriction in trip behavior varies with local crime rate for people of all ages; and whether for the same trip purpose the exposure is different for young and old. Underlying most people's view of crime among the aged is the idea that their vulnerability is what the epidemiologists have called a "host factor" that potentiates the risk of victimization by a criminal who perceives their vulnerability. At this point, this is strictly a hypothesis that is badly in need of testing rather than a self-evident fact.

The perceived threat of crime is just as complex a concept as exposure to crime. On a societal level we know that crime has high salience for many people. The Gallup Poll, for example, found in 1974 that 13 percent of the nation's population, and 21 percent of those living in large cities, named crime as the country's number one problem. Age breakdowns were not available for this belief, but those 50 and over were most likely to express a fear of going outside alone at night.

A current estimate of the extent of fear of crime in the older population was provided by the National Council on the Aging's (1975) survey of a national sample of people 18 and over. About one-quarter of older people considered that crime on the street was a "very serious problem" and stated that this fact significantly limited their mobility. The prevalence of this fear was notably greater than in the case of people under 65. Among the elderly, those with incomes under the poverty threshold expressed more fear than those above; blacks expressed such fear twice as frequently as nonblacks; and women more than men. B.D. Lebowitz (1975) found also that fear was greater among older people living alone than among those with others in a household. Public media have featured reports on crimes, sometimes with emphasis on those whose victims are older people. A crime in one's own neighborhood arouses anxiety in anyone, and this effect is likely to be potentiated where there is a concentration of vulnerable people.

Although we know that people are differentially susceptible to such anxieties, our means of measuring perceived crime threat are not very good. The typical survey method such as that used by the Gallup Poll depends on very brief questions and responses. Even interviews that are more extended and give more of an opportunity for a relationship between interviewer and interviewee to become established are subject to many sources of error. People tend to deny unpleasant feelings; people with a strong need to exhibit mastery may not admit such anxieties; and people may give a minimal estimate of their fear *because* they have already taken into account the fact that they have lowered their risk of exposure by greatly restricting their behavioral space. Thus, we cannot feel that any of the available surveys has provided us with reliable estimates of the magnitude of perceived threat for any age or other subgroup.

A study now in progress by the Philadelphia Geriatric Center and Massachusetts Institute of Technology deals with the three-year survivors of a national sample of elderly tenants in 53 different low-rent public housing environments originally studied by the Philadelphia Geriatric Center in 1971. In the summer of 1974, 662 of these tenants were interviewed so as to obtain extensive information about their behavior and attitudes and about their housing and neighborhood environments. Included in the interview were questions about their personal crime experiences, their knowledge of crimes experienced by other tenants, their feelings of security, and their attitudes and behavior in areas not directly related to crime. Information was also obtained from crime-incident reports from the police district within which their housing was located.

Actual Victimization

Personal crime experience was determined by asking each tenant: "Have you been robbed or attacked during the past three years?" In spite of this specific wording of the question, many of the crimes reported were larceny. Fifteen percent of all tenants reported such an experience, as compared with only 7 percent three years previously. On the first occasion, the time referent was "since you moved here" (an average of 3.9 years), thus increasing the likelihood that the doubling of the rate after three years represented a real increase. The 1974 12-month rate was 7.6 percent. Two-thirds of the criminals who were seen were adolescents, one-quarter adult, and about one-tenth children. Half were committed in the afternoon, a little over a third after 6:00 P.M., and the remainder in the morning. The greatest proportion (40%) occurred in the dwelling unit or in the local neighborhood (30%), with smaller proportions in the public spaces of multiunit buildings or on the grounds of the project. Just under a quarter indicated that they were hurt during the incident. Seventy percent indicated they had reported the crime to the police.

Exposure to Crime

The median total crime rate per 100,000 in the local neighborhoods where the housing projects were located was 10,086, as compared with the national average for 1974 of 4,821 (United States Department of Justice 1974b). Thus these public housing tenants have far greater residential exposure than the average American. There were several indications that our tenants limit their activities in ways that reduce their exposure. A full two-thirds of our sample indicated there were times (primarily at night) when they were afraid to go outside their dwellings. Even more (69 percent) *never* leave their dwellings at night. Almost half (42 percent) said they typically avoided certain locations because they were unsafe. About a quarter of those who use outdoor spaces for sitting avoid certain unsafe places, and a quarter of those who do not sit outdoors are deterred because they consider any available place unsafe. Of course, we do not know how younger people would respond to such questions. It is most unlikely, however, that the proportion never going out at night or afraid to leave their dwellings at night would be this high among younger groups. It does seem clear, then, that exposure to crime is significantly reduced at the expense of a restriction of these older tenants' mobility.

The Fear of Crime

Some of the data on limiting exposure to crime reviewed above implies fear of crime. Other data speak more directly to this issue. Feeling safe is very much a matter of where one is and whether it is day or night. Ninety-four percent felt safe within their dwelling units at all times, as compared with 70 percent within other areas of their multiunit buildings, 41 percent in the outdoor spaces of their housing, and 31 percent in the neighborhood. Two percent *never* feel safe in their dwelling units, 7 percent in their building, 9 percent on the grounds, and 15 percent in the neighborhood. About one-third of the tenants in multistory buildings expressed a fear of using elevators and one-fifth a fear of stairways (most tenants avoid the latter). More than half were able to describe incidents that had happened to fellow tenants.

The status of knowledge thus far on three major crime-related variables may be summarized as follows: The *crime victimization rate* among the elderly is as high or higher than for other groups in two apparently age-related crimes: robbery with injury and larceny with contact. *Exposure to crime* is less well-understood, but indirect evidence suggests strongly that older people limit their exposure by avoiding places they consider dangerous and especially by restricting their range of movement at night. *Fear of crime* is very high, notably more so among the elderly than among younger age groups. Women, those with lower incomes, and blacks are, not surprisingly, more prone to this anxiety.

The meaning of these generalizations for the individual's psychological state may now be considered. Theoretical frameworks developed by R. Lazarus (1966), J. Cassell (1975), and K.K. Schooler (1975) in their stress models for human behavior are useful for this purpose. In this view, the individual deals with the external world by processing information received through sensory channels in terms of its personal meaning for him. This process of *appraisal* attempts to assess an environmental situation in terms of its potential threat. Threat may be perceived either in terms of doubt about the individual's own capacity to deal with the situation or of the magnitude of the threat. If threat is perceived, behavior is modified so as to cope with the threat. This resulting behavior may take a variety of forms from adaptive to nonadaptive, concurrent with alterations in one's inner state. A state of appraised threat is always experienced at some "cost" to the individual in terms of strain or anxiety, in the extreme case leading to psychological or physical symptoms. "Normal" people are by no means immune to such cost. For example, recent research has demonstrated that people who experience major changes in their life situations, such as bereavement, marriage, or change of job, are more likely to develop physical illnesses during the time following the change (Holmes and Masuda 1974). Most people's coping behavior does ultimately lead to the reestablishment of a new equilibrium following the change, so that the strain diminishes or disappears. Some threatening situations are chronic, however, requiring constant vigilance to maintain the behavior designed to cope with the threat.

For the person who lives in a crime-ridden neighborhood, the threat of attack is persistent. The appraisal process rightly calculates the threat as real. If the older person himself has not been a victim of a crime, he is likely to know someone who has been victimized or to have heard about such a person from a friend or through the news media. Theoretically, one should expect the perceived magnitude of threat to be roughly proportional to the crime rate in a given neighborhood.

However, the other standard for appraisal is the individual's assessment of his own ability to deal with the threat, the *host factor* in stress. It should be clear from knowledge of the deprivations associated with growing old that the older person's vulnerability is just as real as the environmental threat, and that most older people are aware of their greater vulnerability. This awareness in the best of times is associated with a devaluation of the self. The same National Council on the Aging (1975) survey mentioned above also documented that, if anything, older people are *more* likely than the young to think negatively about the capacities of the aged as a group. In association with the real threat of crime, an interaction between the environmental threat and the personal vulnerability occurs, so that those who are most vulnerable are likely to be disproportionately negatively affected and to suffer the greatest loss of self-esteem through the realization of this vulnerability.

It is in the coping behavior of the older person that the clearest effect of the threat of crime ought to be seen. Earlier reference has been made to the limited data on how both older and younger people attempt to control their exposure to potential victimization. Taking what is known about older people into account, however, some important ways can be suggested in which the deprivations characteristic of aging may affect the behavior of the older person in coping with the threat of crime:

1. Limitations in visual and auditory acuity may result in a threat being unrecognized. Conversely, in attempting to compensate for such reduced ability to see or hear a potential criminal, some people may become oversensitized to the point of chronic anxiety or paranoid suspiciousness.

2. Even if a threatening situation is perceived correctly, it may not be analyzed correctly in terms of the action demanded. Typically, an attempted crime occurs unexpectedly and in fast sequence, straining the limits of the older person's information-processing capacity. In psychological experiments, the most frequent type of error made by older subjects is the "error of omission," that is, the withholding of a response, rather than the making of an incorrect response (Botwinick 1973). Thus, the older person may simply remain passive when faced with a sudden threat, even when some appropriate aversive maneuver is available. One must recognize, however, that there may be many times when a lack of positive response may be more adaptive than an ill-considered counter-aggressive response.

3. Even if the proper judgment of a situation is made, there are essential limitations on the physical response ability of the older person. A faster walk, running, holding tight to a purse, and so on, simply cannot be accomplished as well with aged muscles or in the presence of the more severe disabilities to which the elderly are prone.

4. Social isolation has a direct effect on the older person's ability to control his exposure to crime. The person living alone in a household is much more vulnerable being required to do errands alone unless a deliberate effort is made to find someone to accompany her.

5. Economic deprivation limits the extent to which safer transportation such as driving an automobile or using a taxi may be used to reduce the risk.

6. The complexly determined change from a personality orientation of active mastery to passive mastery may limit the individual's readiness to make major changes in his life situation that would remove him from a situation of chronic risk. One form of security engendered by remaining in familiar physical surroundings may override willingness to move from a residence in a high-crime neighborhood to one in a better neighborhood even if the move is economically feasible (Lawton, Kleban, and Carlson 1973).

Our research asked explicitly about the measures tenants took to protect themselves from possible victimization. About half could name only one or no such measure, usually consisting of simply locking their doors. All other mechanisms were mentioned only by a scattering of tenants. Techniques that we tend to think of as "typical," such as not carrying money on one's person, was mentioned by 12 tenants out of 662; going out only with other people was mentioned by 13. At least as mentioned in such open-end interview fashion, then, their repertory of coping skills does not seem large.

What is the net adaptive value of this set of coping behaviors? It appears to be a probable reduction in victimization at the expense of richness of life-style, such as the freedom to visit friends and relatives, to sit in outdoor locations, to participate in the free activities of the city, or to traverse the neighborhood. For those who are most vulnerable physically, psychologically, or economically, access to basic, life-maintaining resources such as shopping and medical care may be blocked. The acute experience of threat is thus reduced, but the loss in other areas is great. Since these losses are apt to block the satisfaction of important social and psychological needs, the cost to the individual persists, whether it be in direct deprivation, loss of self-esteem, or conversion into psychological or physical symptoms.

We do not mean to suggest that all older people are passive, helpless, and paralyzed by fear. Our data on individual tenants show clearly how resilient and masterful the majority are, even many of those who have been personally victimized. However, all who are potential victims are at greater psychological risk, and the perceived threat in the absence of really effective coping behavior may well be the critical factor in their ability to live satisfying lives.

References

Botwinick, J. 1973. *Aging and behavior.* New York: Springer.

Cassel, J. 1975. The relation of the urban environment to health: Toward a

29

conceptual frame and a research strategy. Mimeo report. Chapel Hill: University of North Carolina, School of Medicine.

Gallup Poll. 1973. Special report on crime in the United States. *Gallup Opinion Index*, Report No. 91, January.

Golant, S.M. 1972. *The residential location and spatial behavior of the elderly.* Research Paper No. 143. Chicago: University of Chicago, Geography Department.

Holmes, T.H., and Masuda, M. 1974. Life change and illness susceptibility. In Dohrenwend, B.S., and B.P. Dohrenwend (eds.). *Stressful life events.* New York: Wiley.

Lawton, M.P., Kleban, M.H., and Carlson, D.A. 1973. The inner-city resident: To move or not to move. *Gerontologist*, 13, 443-448.

Lazarus, R. 1966. *Psychological stress and the coping process.* New York: McGraw-Hill.

Lebowitz, B.D. 1975. Age and fearfulness: Personal and situational factors. *Journal of Gerontology*, 30, 696-700.

National Council on the Aging. 1975. *The myth and reality of aging in America.* Washington, D.C.: National Council on the Aging.

Neugarten, B.L., and associates. 1964. *Personality in middle and late life.* New York: Atherton.

Rotter, J.B. 1966. Generalized expectancies for internal versus external control of reinforcement. *Psychological Monographs*, 80, 1 (Whole No. 609).

Schaie, K.W. 1974. Translations in gerontology—from lab to life: Intellectual functioning. *American Psychologist*, 29, 802-807.

Schooler, K.K. 1975. Response of the elderly to environment: A stress-theoretical perspective. In Windley, P.G., T.O. Byerts, and F.G. Ernst (eds.). *Theory development in environment and aging.* Washington, D.C.: Gerontological Society.

Shanas, E. 1971. Measuring the home health needs of the aged in five countries. *Journal of Gerontology*, 26, 37-40.

United States Department of Justice. 1974a. *Crime in eight American cities.* Washington, D.C.: U.S. Department of Justice.

United States Department of Justice. 1974b. *Crime in the United States.* Washington, D.C.: U.S. Department of Justice.

United States Department of Justice. 1975. *Criminal victimization surveys in thirteen American cities.* Washington, D.C.: U.S. Department of Justice.

4 Pattern and Effect of Crime Against the Aging: The Kansas City Study

Carl L. Cunningham

I have lost my professional detachment on the subjects of how crimes are being committed against the elderly American, why something more should be done about it, and what that something might be. I view the problem now as a great deal more serious and far more resistant to even partial solution than I did three years ago when we commenced the research.

The hard fact is that crime is devastating the lives of thousands of relatively defenseless older Americans. Harder, and even sadder, facts are that many public officials and private citizens are unaware that a special problem exists, or they choose not to believe the evidence of its existence. But perhaps most discouraging is the gaping disparity between what we know about the problem of crime and what we seem to be able to do about it.

Criminal behavior is highly differentiated, a fact we also tend to ignore. Crime is not a "thing," it is a complex skein of acts, violated values, and adverse outcomes. A criminal act does not always benefit the offender; but it usually deprives someone. Therefore, for purposes of this discussion, I refer to crime generally in the sense of a system of social and economic deprivation. Thought of that way, it is easier to assess the magnitude of its ultimate effect on the elderly population.

As a country, we are weary of grappling with problems that defy our conventional remedy of money—and crime is in the vanguard of such defiance. A few years ago, one could still discern hope among knowledgeable people that technology transfer to law enforcement operations, together with sizeable increases in police forces, would put a tactical damper on the crime fire. But they have not dampened it much; although it is certainly possible that we would have been much worse off had we not spent the huge sums and taken the actions we did. We seem now to accept, generally, the long-standing conviction of many social and behavioral scientists that crime is rooted in the virtual soul of a society, emanating, among other things, from maldistributions of the good things of life, inequities of opportunity, sometimes of ability, but all made explicit by our excellent system of communications. As a society, we tend also toward increasingly higher levels of stimulation seeking, of which violence and overconsumption are usually integral parts.

This immensely complex scheme of contributing factors, coupled with our historical inability to significantly reduce and control crime, has created an atmosphere that shows signs of a beginning public acceptance of crime and the deprivations that attend it. At the same time, in the centers of research and professionalism most concerned with crime and related problems, and in some areas of the public sector, there seems to be an increasing tendency to point to the ills of the society—not alone in the sense of their being the root causes of crime, but sometimes in the sense that we deserve the criminal and the results of his acts seeing that we conduce him. Without trying to disprove that line of thinking, it is fair to say that it has contributed something to our notable lack of social concern for the plight of the crime victim.

The very complexity of the problem of controlling crime, coupled with our conviction that basic social and economic correction is needed in order to accomplish anything permanent and significant, may have caused us to adopt a waiting posture for the miracle of social change. To the extent that the American public has put itself in a holding pattern while "they" "solve" the crime problem by the more indirect means, to about that extent is public participation in action programs aimed at immediately softening the crime problem downgraded.

What I have to say here largely concerns the more immediate, direct action level. That certainly does not mean that I assume such action to be superior to the longer range and more comprehensive corrections of the contributing causes of crime. The proposition as to how crime should be reduced does not involve the simplistics of either the long-range or the immediate-action approach. However, *we are well into a crisis situation concerning the criminal victimization of the elderly who live in or near the higher crime areas of cities.* The density of the elderly population in such areas is steadily increasing. We do not have the leisure to postpone the admittedly discouraging business of trying to help elderly persons avoid being victims (and multiple victims) of crime; trying to reduce the physical aloneness of elderly persons, which is so conducive to their vulnerability; trying to improve the safety of neighborhoods through collective private action; trying to improve police awareness of the special vulnerabilities and fears of the elderly resident of high crime areas, and trying to assess whether, after all such efforts, we are doing any good or making any progress.

I am discussing these matters primarily from the perspective of a study at Midwest Research Institute of serious crimes committed against persons over 60 years of age in Kansas City, Missouri. In the three years since that study began, nearly 6,000 criminal acts committed in Kansas City, Missouri against persons over age 60 have been studied. Of that number, over 1,800 were studied in detail, developing primary data through interviews with victims, next of kin, police, witnesses, and a number of volunteer ex-felons who were known to have accumulated experience in the types of crimes that affected the elderly most seriously. These were residential burglary, armed and strong arm robbery, and larceny.

A breakdown of these cases by type offense is shown in Table 4-1. Fifty-six percent were burglaries, about 25 percent robberies, 13 percent larcenies, and the remainder were assaults-homicides and rapes. Had we attempted to study all

Table 4-1
Breakdown by Type Offense of 1,831 Crimes Against the Elderly

	Number	Percent
Burglary	1,024	55.9
Robbery	450	24.6
Larceny[a]	256	13.9
Assault	45	2.5
Fraud	42	2.3
Rape	5	0.3
Homicide	4	0.2
Other	5	0.3
Total	1,831	100.0

Note: The above crimes, all of which involved victims of age 60 or over, were reported to the Kansas City Missouri Police Department during the approximate period September 1, 1972 to February 1974. They do not constitute all crimes committed against persons of that age category. However, with the exception of larceny, they constitute all crimes in the respective offense categories not committed by a member of the victim's immediate household or family and not involving any ostensible culpability on the victim's part, such as an assault arising from drunken conduct, or gambling, or any circumstances that cast doubt on the true nature of the offense.

[a]Includes many nonviolent purse snatches.

the larcenies, we would simply have been overwhelmed; therefore, we had to select only the major cases, and the purse snatches that, if they are nonviolent, classify as larcenies in Missouri.

Our research supports strongly the initial assumption that, of all persons who become targets of a criminal act, the elderly usually suffer most. There are some very basic reasons for this. Like many other Americans who are victims of crime, the elderly victims are usually poor, both relatively and absolutely. However, they usually have relatively less physical and emotional resiliency than their younger counterparts. Thus, physical and psychic injury resulting from crime can leave a more lasting mark. Many of the elderly who were victimized live alone. In the Kansas City study, more than 60 percent of the burglary victims lived alone; and many stated they knew no one in the neighborhood on whom they felt they could rely for aid.

Although the aging person is somewhat less often criminally victimized, considering the population of a metropolitan area as a whole, that is not a very informative comparison. The elderly living in or near certain neighborhoods of Kansas City, Missouri, for example, can be as much as eight times more vulnerable to serious crimes such as robbery, burglary or major larcenies than a younger resident of a relatively safe suburb who works and shops in areas with low crime rates. This disparity is all the more significant considering the fact that most older Americans live generally circumspect and conservative lives. They are usually active avoiders of crime-conducive situations. Their special vulnerabilities stem primarily from the fact that economic and social changes have tended to concentrate the elderly population of a metropolitan area where there are relatively high numbers of unemployed male youths who are dropouts from school. Thus, they are in close contact with precisely that element of society most likely to criminally victimize them.

However, as important as any of these considerations is the one that over 80 percent of the serious crimes we studied were committed against the elderly persons in their homes or in the immediate vicinity. This is largely a function of burglary being the predominant crime, as it is against Americans of all ages. However, between 50 and 60 percent of the assaults, robberies, and thefts were also committed in or near the home.

Why emphasize where the crime is committed? I believe the answer relates primarily to the primitive social tenant that the home place is sanctuary. Criminal invasion of it, regardless of the outcome or loss, usually assumes larger dimensions in the victim's mind than a crime or accident that occurs elsewhere. Our public concept of safety may therefore be a little too restrictive relating as it does primarily to physical injury, physical threat, and property loss. I suggest that a safe neighborhood is one in which the resident's sense of security and peace of mind are not subject to repeated disruption; and one in which there is confidence on the part of residents that they can deal with contingencies. Above all there must be freedom of movement and choice of actions open to the resident. In a great number of neighborhoods in the United States, those attributes of safety are lacking. The elderly residents are often the ones who feel that lack first and most acutely.

The following, based on the findings of the MRI study, considers first the demographic profiles of the elderly crime victims. Figure 4-1 shows the age groups of the victims of 1,831 serious crimes—homicide, assault, robbery, burglary, larceny, fraud, and rape.

The median age of these victims was 68.8 years. However, the median ages of black crime victims was 66.3 years, no doubt reflecting differences in longevity of the races. The large grouping in the 60-64-year age block was to be expected. However, we did not anticipate the extreme age of some of the victims. More than 12 percent were over 80 years of age. One of these was a black, 84-year-old widow who was the victim of a multiple rape.

Here we differentiate by the race of the victim on the factors of sex, whether they live alone, annual income, physical handicaps, and the type of dwelling structure (Figure 4-2).

The 1970 census for Jackson County, Missouri, in which most of these crimes were committed, counted about 74 percent white to 25 percent black, 1 percent other. Thus, there were about the same proportions of white and black victims of serious crime as there are whites and blacks in the county population at large. However, the white victims are principally those who are living in or

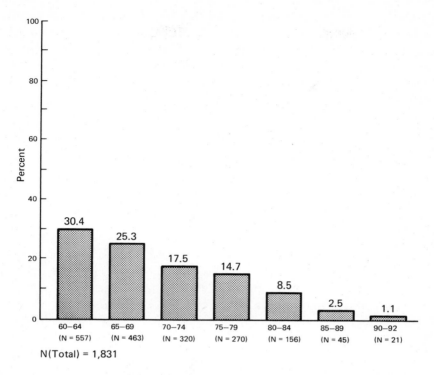

Figure 4-1. Age Distribution of 1,831 Elderly Victims of Serious Crimes.

near the high crime areas of the city. There is definitely not a homogeneous distribution of the crimes affecting whites—as you no doubt would have expected.

The living arrangements of the victims of both races, that is whether they live alone and the type dwelling they occupy, were practically identical, as were the number who were physically handicapped. It is very significant that the victims included 20 and 21 percent, respectively, who had serious physical handicaps—great difficulty in walking and joint movement, impairment of hearing, and visual acuity were the most common.

The similarity in the victim's housing arrangements is influenced by the fact that a large number of white and black crime victims live in the same areas of the city.

Of particular interest are the income levels. Figure 4-3 reflects a sad combination of two facts: first, that the elderly have little income; second, that those who have the least are the most vulnerable to criminal action. Summarizing the arithmetic, we can see that one out of every five black victims of

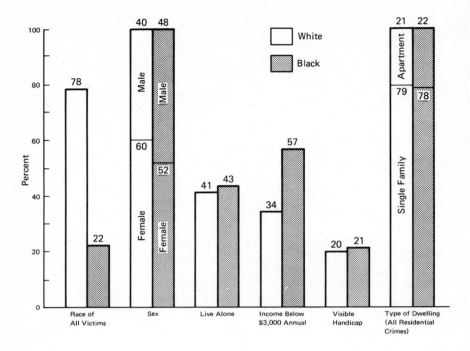

Figure 4-2. Profile of Elderly Victims by Race.

serious crime has an income of less than 1,000 dollars a year. Of the whole group of black victims, about 68 percent have incomes of less than $3,000 annually. The situation is a little better with the white victims—but not much. Considering black and white victims together, 47 percent have incomes of less than $3,000. All these income figures include family units, where applicable.

Twelve percent of the respondents would not report their incomes. Judging from the places of residence—and the median incomes of the appropriate census tract—there does not seem to have been any significant clustering of nonrespondents in any one income category. However, slightly more seem to have been in the over $10,000 bracket than in others.

Considering crimes from the point of view of race of the elderly victim (Figure 4-4), we see that the percentages of burglary, assault and rape, and fraud committed against white and black persons are fairly close to the percentages of whites and blacks in the population of Jackson County itself—which is 74 and 25 percent white and black, respectively.

However, these data indicate that elderly whites are being robbed at a higher

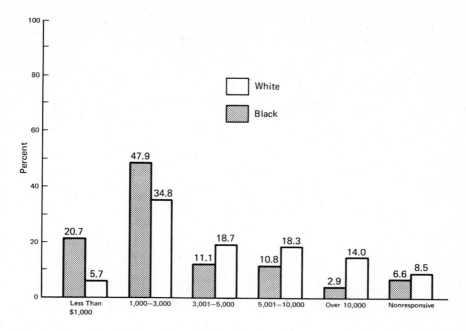

Figure 4-3. Annual Income Distribution by Race of All Elderly Victims Studied.

rate than blacks, proportionate to population, and they are more often victims of larceny. On the other hand, these may be only a seeming disparity, brought about by black victims being less reluctant to report crimes against them to the police.

The broad economic effects of property crimes on the victim population is a critical issue.

From Figure 4-5 you can see in more detail the way robbery, burglary, and larceny victims are distributed as far as their income is concerned. Over 58 percent of the robbery victims had incomes under $5,000 a year, and the situation is generally worse with respect to burglary and larceny victims.

Let us consider the more specific effects of these losses on the victims in the lower income categories. The median loss suffered by the robbery victims was about $39. That is, half lost more than $39, half of them lost less. From burglary the median was $97 and from larceny about $24. Consider a hypothetical, but very realistic, example of a widow living on $1,500 a year who loses $39 in cash from a robbery. That loss amounts to 2.6 percent of her annual income, which does not seem severe. By direct comparison to someone earning $15,000 a year, it equates to $390.

But that would not be a fair comparison because in both cases we have

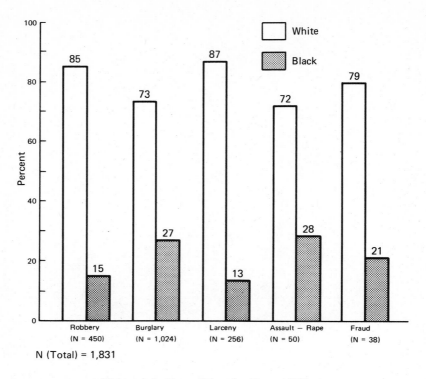

Figure 4-4. Type Crime by Race of Victim.

considered the problem on the basis of annual income. Few people, and certainly not the poor, have the financial resiliency to absorb losses over a long term. The elderly poor live mostly on a monthly budget—conforming to the social security payments. Therefore, to understand the real effect of this $39 loss, and its comparable loss to a person of higher income, we must put the problem on a monthly basis. The loss is then 31 percent of her total monthly income. Every dollar of that loss cuts into necessities. She is very unlikely to have any margin. She can absorb the cut only through denial of basic commodities and necessary services. Now compare the situation of the $15,000-a-year wage earner. We assess him a 31 percent cut too—or the $390. But is the effect really the same? The answer is "no." We may safely assume that he has a little margin in his budget. At least he has alternatives open to him—loans, extended credit, help from employers, perhaps insurance, if not savings. The elderly widow in our example is far less likely to have such alternatives open to her. That is what relative deprivation by criminal acts is all about.

39

Figure 4-5. Income of Robbery, Burglary, and Larceny Victims.

The problems of economic loss, the fear of injury, and the general withdrawal associated with these crimes is greatly compounded by the fact that many of the victims we have been discussing have suffered repeatedly.

Of the 1,518 elderly victims of robbery, burglary, and larceny (Table 4-2), over 26 percent were multiple victims. The overwhelming majority of persons who were multiple victims of crime were victimized in the same way as the first time. For example, robbery victims tended to be robbed again rather than burglarized. There is strong inference here that the pattern of the victim's life make him more or less vulnerable to one type offense than another.

It is important to note some of the changes victims have reported in their living habits shortly after the crimes were committed against them. The most drastic reaction is abandonment of the home. We have had several reports of that following a burglary or robbery. But probably more important, nearly 40 percent of the persons victimized by burglary and robbery reported they no longer go to certain places, or engage in some activities because of fear induced by crime. About 40 percent of the burglary victims stated they had active expectations their homes would be broken into before it happened.

There is also notable a deep pessimism among the victims of both races who live in the high crime areas concerning their ability to protect themselves and their property—and they express particularly adverse reactions toward youths of both races. This is not surprising because the elderly who are living in the areas

Table 4-2
Multiple Victims of Crime

Offense	Number	Percent
Robbery		
Multiple victim	85	23.6
Not a multiple victim	275	76.5
Total	360	100.0
Burglary		
Multiple victim	253	29.2
Not a multiple victim	613	70.8
Total	866	100.0
Larceny		
Multiple victim	44	19.9
Not a multiple victim	177	80.1
Total	221	100.0
All victims		
Multiple victim	405	26.7
Not a multiple victim	1,113	73.3
Total	1,518	100.0

where there are largest numbers of unemployed school dropouts are facing conditions not only detrimental to their physical security, but to the whole quality of their lives.

To cite an example, I was called by an 84-year-old woman, infirm and living alone in a public housing development, whose social security money had been stolen twice in the preceding four months. She was positive the thieves were the teenage children of families living in the same apartment house. She told me that she had no money, and was afraid she was starving because she had eaten only a few boiled potatoes in the past ten days. We called the welfare authorities, and she was helped. But her condition and her location will combine to keep her vulnerable unless something extraordinary is done.

Considering the offenders, the most salient fact in this study is perhaps that the young American is attacking, stealing from, and generally victimizing the old. This is no doubt largely because the American male under about age 24 commits the majority of so-called "street" crime. However, the element of vulnerability and physical juxtaposition of the elderly poor and the unemployed crime-prone youths is also a very significant factor.

As you can see (Figure 4-6), over half of all suspects developed in the 1,831 cases we studied were known or estimated to have been still in their teens. This does not mean they were all juveniles—which are legally defined in Missouri as those under 17. Thus, when we speak of those older than 17, they are—by definition of law at any rate—young adult offenders. Another 24 percent of the suspects were in their twenties. Therefore, the overwhelming majority of suspects developed—77 percent specifically—were younger than 30. Burglars tended to be younger than robbers, perhaps because robbery takes a little more courage and preparation. Some of that preparation is purse snatching, which is classified as a larceny if it does not result in violence to the person or the victim.

The known offenders or suspects were predominantly black, particularly where robbery was concerned (Figure 4-7). It is important to note that this chart shows only the percentage breakdown by racial categories of suspects developed. Obviously, in the majority of burglary cases, there was no suspect developed at all. There is an unknown category as far as race of the offender is concerned, even in robbery, because some victims were attacked in the dark, from behind, or were simply too shaken to remember. One aged widow died from a beating given her by a man she never saw. He struck her from behind while she was watching television in her home.

Consider one of the more critical aspects of the problem. The average American has not had much opportunity—or at least much stimulus—to think of the acts we loosely describe as "street crime" as an operational system. But criminal acts have a tactical setting and method attendant to them that is a fertile field for the investigator bent on discovering how certain offenses can be deterred, or prevented. There are basically four factors or forces operating in the criminal act to provide it a tactical setting.

42

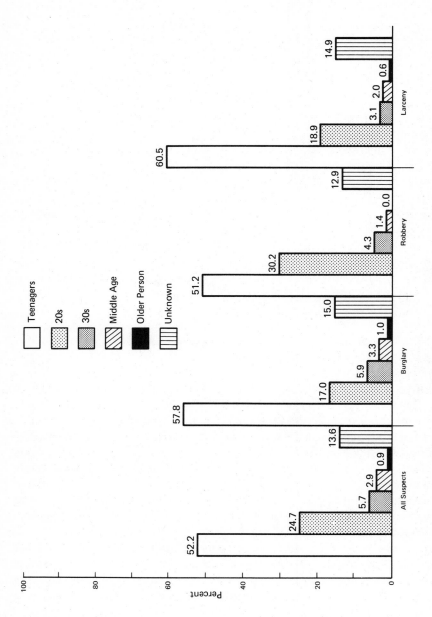

Figure 4-6. Age of Offenders (Cases in Which Suspects Developed).

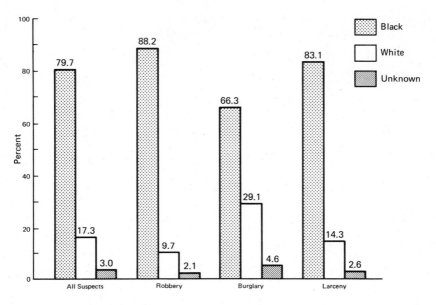

Figure 4-7. Race of Offenders.

1. The target or the victim
2. The offender
3. The manpower and resources that society places in the field to deter or apprehend an offender
4. The general physical and social environment in which the offense is committed

By tactical setting I am referring to the nature and arrangement of the physical environment in which the crime is committed. It also refers to the entire pattern of small-scale actions and events that influence the commission of the crime or its avoidance.

Within that tactical setting, the criminal invariably has great opening advantage. He has the initiative. He can decide the time, the setting, the place, the victims, the method, and how much risk he will take in committing the crime; and almost to the last second he can decide whether he will go through with it. In numerous interviews with some very experienced and hardened ex-felons, I was repeatedly impressed with how powerful an influence this factor of initiative was in the successful completion of a crime.

On the other hand, the citizen—the prospective victim—must set up his defenses on the basis of what he perceives as the threat; but, invariably, he lacks complete knowledge. Sometimes he perceives no threat at all when a great one actually exists. He seldom has sufficient resources to cover more than a few of the contingencies. Thus, his defensive preparations, if any, are a system of compromises and trade-offs. Personal and residential security are therefore set essentially as an adversary condition between the persons attempting to protect something and those who may attempt to victimize them.

For example, consider the tactical situation commonly involved with the burglary of a house or apartment (Figure 4-8). There are great differences in the two setups—shown in the figure, but they also have important things in common.

I have established some arbitrary zone boundaries for each. Zone I is the beginning of the private property line—the area in both cases where a prospective burglar commences to make himself at least theoretically vulnerable when he crosses it. Zone II is the point at which penetration usually creates suspicion and danger for the offender. Virtually anyone can approach along the public thoroughfare without creating suspicion. But note that in the apartment building, the larger the public area and the more entrances that can be used that are not under surveillance the easier it is to penetrate the building without arousing suspicion.

In the private residence, on the other hand, any penetration of the private property line raises the possibility of occupant or neighborhood alertness, if not actual suspicion.

There are two simple points here—but important ones.

1. There are certain actions the offender must usually risk to gain his objective, for example, penetration of a dwelling space in some way to commit a burglary.
2. The general nature of our organized physical environment usually poses some widely recognized boundaries, the penetration of which should, if the society is alert, greatly heighten the vulnerability of the intruder to suspicion, if not apprehension.

Unfortunately, the social fragmentation of neighborhoods, particularly in the higher crime areas of a city, makes that second point more a theory than a fact.

Americans are prone to ignore one another, even in time of need. I suspect this is also an international problem. However, that propensity is certainly marked where crime threatens most and ironically where it can do the most harm. If an offender can approach a private residence, make a forcible entry, a quick cleanout, and then get away with some assurance that, even if he was seen by one of his victim's neighbors, he will not be reported, the tactical balance I referred to earlier shifts dramatically in his favor. The boldness evident in the tactics of hundreds of burglary cases we studied indicates that neighborhood indifference—in a few cases actual complicity—has provided the criminal precisely that sort of advantage. That is the sort of advantage that police are virtually powerless to counterbalance on their own.

The criminal usually has a fairly good tactical perception, which means a sense of how best to apply force to achieve his objective, to use time to his advantage, to take steps to reduce his own vulnerability while exploiting the vulnerability and weaknesses of his target. But above all, he is interested in the tactics of his principal opponent—the police.

I have interviewed a number of young ex-felons, and the overwhelming majority of them struck me as having a good grasp of police operations and capabilities. They are seldom far wrong in their estimates of minimum average response times in a given part of the city, how dense the patrol activity is, and what factors or indicators are most likely to trigger a patrol unit's suspicion. They recognize, with a far greater degree of perception than does the average citizen, the fundamental constraints placed on law enforcement agencies—particularly in the patrol activity.

We are fond of pointing out how the automobile has revolutionized police patrol. It is true that cars allow wider and faster patrol. They also reduce the size of the force needed to cover a given amount of ground. But while making the patrol more mobile, the automobile has also made it largely a function of the street. The attention is largely on the street because they are drivers primarily. They must devote at least 75 percent of their attention to moving the car safely through traffic. The remainder of their attention span is keyed to the unusual event or noise, to the extent that those can be filtered out from the ambient levels. But primarily the patrol officer reacts to the orders of a dispatcher who, in turn, reacts to reports and complaints.

There is insignificant probability that a patrol unit will come past the residence being burglarized at precisely the time when the offender is making some overt move that would call attention to himself. Even when this does occasionally occur, the patrol may often miss the significance of what he sees, for the simple reason that the offender is acutely aware of his vulnerability at such a time and does little that would draw attention when a patrol car is in the vicinity. He is, in fact, far more fearful of the powers of observation of neighbors than of police; but that fear is not particularly justified by neighbors' actions. Of the 1,024 burglaries of residences studied in detail in this project, over 60 percent were committed during daylight hours using the front or back door or first floor windows as the point of entry. Half of these burglaries involved the use of force to make the entry-shattering glass, prying doors, breaking door frames, and the like. Practically none of these crimes was reported by either a neighbor or a passerby who would have had an excellent chance of observing the act in progress.

The implication here is for a new focus of social concern and cooperation in combatting the threat to public safety in American neighborhoods. One of the lessons of that sad debacle in Vietnam was that even the most elaborate

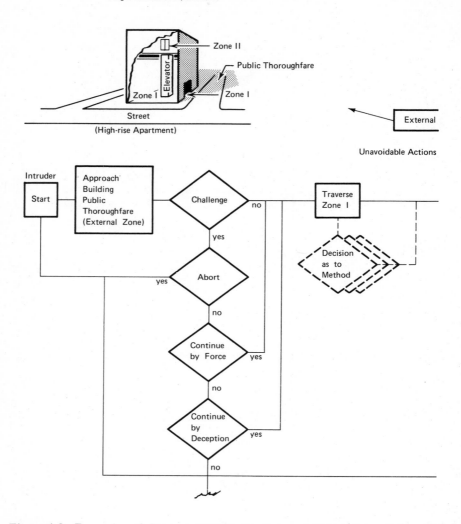

Figure 4-8. Example of Protected Unit Zoning and Patterning of Intruder Actions Based on Common Characteristics and Unavoidable Actions.

electronic sensors and surveillance systems were virtually useless against determined infiltrators; but that reports of people of what was happening were usually of an effective means of counteracting infiltration. In the final analysis, all burglars and robbers are infiltrators, and most are pretty skilled at it. The police, in short, need an alert and cooperative citizenry to fight

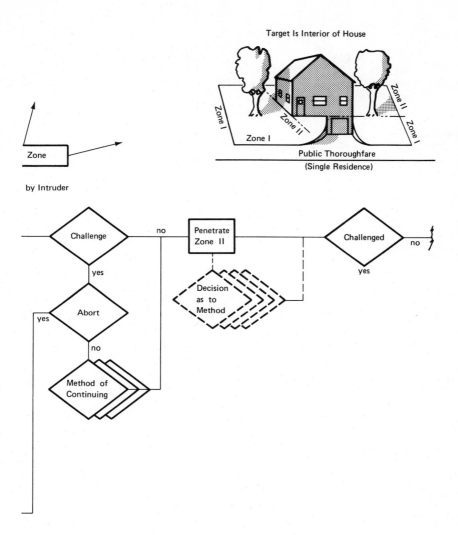

Target Is Interior of House

Zone II

Zone I

Zone I

Zone II

Zone I

Zone II

Zone I

Public Thoroughfare
(Single Residence)

Zone

by Intruder

crime in neighborhoods far more than they need more hardware or man-power.

Probably because the blood and gore of television has conditioned us to think in physically violent terms when crime is mentioned, it is useful to consider here that residential burglary is the principal threat to the elderly citizen, as it is to most Americans. I believe that purse snatches, both of the so-called nonviolent and violent type (the latter being robbery), follow as a fear producer among elderly women. These two crimes, residential burglary and purse snatching, are the principal deprivers.

Burglary is not only the most prevalent serious crime committed against the aging American, it is exceptionally hard to prevent or to solve. The burglar is committing his crime, technically at least, against a place rather than a person. He actively attempts to avoid human contact. He is thus more than usually sensitive to evidence of occupancy, of being observed and possibly reported out of suspicion, and of being surprised in the process of his crime.

But burglary also takes time to commit. It seems safe to estimate that the average stay time of a burglar inside the premises of his target will be approximately 12 minutes. Many stay much longer, of course. This stay time theoretically allows the police more opportunity for on-site apprehension than for most other type crimes.

The burglars we interviewed unanimously reported themselves as under great stress when working. The longer the stay time the greater the stress. A burglar is almost always dangerous, in spite of the essentially fugitive nature of his crime, and particularly so to anyone he unexpectedly encounters during the commission of the burglary. There is strong evidence that two of the homicides of elderly persons we studied resulted from unexpected encounters with a burglar. But the essential point here is not the exact character of the offense, or the way it is technically classified under the law. In the real, operative sense of the victim's view of the matter, burglary is a fear producer of an order about that of night-time street robbery. Elderly victims of residential burglary, almost without exception, displayed a long-lasting residual fear that obviously emanated from a sense of anonymous invasion and latent threat.

The offense commonly referred to as purse snatching is not legally defined as such. It is either a larceny or a robbery, depending on the nature of its commission. However, it is important to remember that this offense, and others, can easily escalate or translate from one level of seriousness to another. Just as an intended burglary can become a murder, so can an intended nonviolent purse snatch result in serious injury or death. A purse snatch by a 14-year-old boy resulted in prolonged hospitalization of a woman in her late seventies for a broken pelvis. Another elderly woman died from a blow to the head struck after she resisted having her purse taken. Obviously, there are no neat dividing lines between one type offense and another.

The pattern of the purse snatch offenses is in some ways significantly different from others. This offense exhibits strongly the insidious characteristic of the young preying on the old in the neighborhood. There is also evidence here that, at least as far as the Kansas City situation is concerned, the elderly white woman is the special target of the young black offender. About 85 percent of all purse snatches were committed against white women. Of the offenders, 84 percent were black. Ninety-five percent were males, practically all of whom were known or estimated to be in their teens or early twenties.

The victims were generally older than the study's victim population at large, probably because of the greater longevity of women more than any other factor. Seventy-four percent of the victims were living alone, and about a third of them were injured in some way. Two deaths resulted from this offense. The purse snatches were more often committed in the victim's neighborhood than any other place. A surprising number occurred inside buildings. About 10 percent occurred inside the victims' homes; and another 17 percent were committed inside a public building or store. Bus stops were also a favorite target area.

Generally, the women who were victim of a purse snatch or strong armed robbery seem to have had relatively little prior perception of exactly how such offenses are committed and what the danger signals are. In fact, this statement could be made to apply to a large number of victims and offense situations.

With that admittedly sketchy outline of the pattern of the offenses that were committed against the elderly in one midwestern city, it is clear that the situation is serious. The fundamental question is what counteractions seem likely to pay off in the short run? To say we must get the public involved sounds platitudinous, and I do not suggest that as an answer in itself. There are means, admittedly laborious and fraught with a very considerable amount of frustration, by which citizen volunteer groups can significantly aid the elderly avoid crime. Public information, home visits, telephone reassurances, police talks to groups, special surveys to identify the elderly recluse being terrified by crime or the threat of it—all of these actions have their purpose and none are very effective taken singly. Alexis deTocqueville, during his famous visit to America in the nineteenth century noted and later commented at length in his *Democracy in America* that wherever there are more than a handful of Americans, they commence to organize. I do not recall, however, that he critiqued our propensity to organize sometimes to little purpose, while ignoring a pressing need for cohesive action in some less palatable sector. The neighborhood crime problem seems definitely to be one of the latter.

I would like to outline the work that has been done thus far in Kansas City to model a citizen volunteer group specifically oriented and trained to aid the elderly, both the crime victim and nonvictim.

Midwest Research Institute combined forces last year with the Shephards Center, a very effective and vital organization that extends a number of educational and personal services to the elderly in Kansas City, Missouri. Operating on the results of this study, MRI staff has been training Shephards Center volunteers who, through telephone contacts and home visits, attempt to transfer some useful information on crime-avoidance measures. The center, with MRI help, has produced a professional home security measures handbook designed specifically for this purpose, and a program is now underway to train elderly volunteers to conduct professional-level home security checks that will be offered free to the elderly public. MRI staff members give numerous public presentations, including TV and radio. The entire thrust of the program is of a practical nature, emphasizing how the citizens—the elderly citizens—can help themselves.

A critical aspect of neighborhood and individual self-help is knowing what constitutes suspicious activity. Police are frequently frustrated by the vague reports of citizens who have had ample time to observe closely a criminal act, but who concentrate on the trivial and nonessential elements of the crime and come away unable to report what could be definite identifying information. The Shephards Center Project and information is also oriented on the suspicious activity indicators.

The project has the full and active cooperation of the Kansas City Police Department. Therefore, information being disseminated does not conflict with the police perspective. The volunteer group in no way supplants police efforts, nor are they in any way involved in police investigation, police auxiliary work, or the like. I would like to be able to say definitely what effect such efforts as this have on the grim picture I was forced to paint for you. Unless this type of effort spreads, and spreads widely both in Kansas City and nationally, I am afraid nothing more can be said of it than that it was laudable, and that it supplied useful information and experience. But if it can be spread, not necessarily in any precise form, but at least with the same general thrust, intent, and content, it will be one of the more significant advances in the private sector's attempts to grapple with street crimes.

However, in the long run, no programmatic approach will avail much in suppressing residential crime unless there is active public commitment not only to action but to the basic idea that a crime against one member of a community threatens the common, as well as the individual, weal. In spite of a national outcry against crime, that idea still seems to be curiously inert at the grass roots of American society.

5

The Urban Elderly:
Environments of Fear

Richard A. Sundeen
and *James T. Mathieu*

The purpose of this chapter is to report the findings of an exploratory study into some of the physical and social environments that invoke or reduce the fear of criminal victimization among elderly. The data was collected from older persons living in nonpublic housing—condominiums, apartments, and single-family residences—in three communities in southern California. In reporting the study, the following questions are answered:

1. What are the physical and social environments of the three groups?
2. What are the levels of perceived safety and fear of crime?
3. What precautions does each group take as a response to its situations?
4. What are the relationships between personal situations, perceptions of safety, and fear of crime?
5. What sorts of policy and action measures aimed at reducing the fear of crime might be suggested by the findings?

Background

A limited number of studies have been made regarding the salient conditions underlying the fear of crime and there is agreement in the findings that ". . . the fear of crime is not a consequence of direct experiences as a victim" (Boggs 1971, p. 22; see also Ennis 1967; McIntyre 1967; and Conklin 1971). These studies suggest that the intensity of concern about crime varies according to social characteristics, such as race, sex, and income level, for example, black women have the highest degree of anxiety, followed in order by black men, white women, and white men, and lower income levels have greater anxiety than higher levels (Ennis 1967, pp. 72-79); parenthood, for example, parents have higher fear of crime in specific situations than their youth (Savitz 1972); location of residence, for example, more central-city residents are apt to feel that violent crime is likely to happen and fewer see their neighborhood as being safe than suburban or rural residents (Boggs 1971).

As for responses to fearful situations, John E. Conklin (1971) distinguishes between *direct victimization* (where loss is "incurred by the victim in such

A portion of this chapter appeared in *The Gerontologist*, 16 no. 3, June, 1976, under the title "The Fear of Crime and Its Consequences Among Elderly in Three Urban Communities."

'crimes with victims' as murder, rape, robbery, and burglary") and *indirect victimization* (where "an individual may suffer a loss from a crime in which he is not directly involved"). Thus, the attitudes and behavior (such as a sense of personal safety, interpersonal trust, and feelings toward one's community) of individuals not directly victimized may be changed to the extent that an increase in the amount of crime around them occurs and/or is perceived. Elsewhere Conklin (1975) suggests that fear of crime is divisive and nonintegrative to communities. Related to responses to the perception and fear of crime, Sarah L. Boggs (1971) found that residents of the central city, in contrast to rural-small town and suburban samples, tended to depend less upon police for assistance, were less satisfied with police protection, and were more likely to take "special precautions" out of concern for crime. Also, Richard L. Block (1971) found the fear of police to be a more important determinant of support for police than fear of crime.

Although there has been some documentation that the elderly are concerned about crime, for example, a 1972 national survey of 70,000 persons over the age of 52 indicated that high crime ranked second to inflation as the most critical problem facing the United States (*Los Angeles Times* 1973), this does not necessarily mean there is extraordinary fear of it. Frank Furstenburg (1971) distinguishes between a concern about crime, which is related to resentment of changing social conditions, and a fear of victimization based on their perceptions of safety in their local neighborhoods.

Jaber Gubrium (1974, p. 250) hypothesizes that if elderly live in areas where there exist "comparatively extensive friendships among socially concentrated aged persons . . . they will have socially sympathetic and supportive relationships which diffuse their fears." In turn, in age-heterogeneous areas where such supportive relationships are not as common, isolates will have to deal with their fear of being victimized individually without many "locally supportive relationships," thus causing fears to be magnified. Further, it is likely that persons who must face their perceived problem of possible victimization alone will take greater precautions to minimize the risks than those who have a sense of social support.

With these studies in mind, data was collected that would describe the social contexts and consequences of the fear of crime among elderly in three communities in southern California. The primary concepts that were explored and compared were (1) the degree of social support, (2) the perception of safety in the neighborhood, (3) the fear of specific crimes, and (4) security precautions taken.

Methodology

Three areas in southern California were selected that represent three types of urban neighborhoods where elderly typically reside—central city (*Core*), an urban municipality (*Slurb*), and a retirement community (*Retirement*). Samples were selected on an availability basis in two areas (regular members of senior citizen clubs in Core ($N = 26$) and Slurb ($N = 28$)) and by random selection from the Retirement ($N = 50$) telephone directory. The data were collected through an interview schedule that took between 30 and 60 minutes to complete, and included several attitudinal questions asked in conjunction with an 11-inch thermometer—like scale made out of cardboard. The scale was calibrated by tens from 0 to 100, with "high," "medium," and "low" marked along the side of the scale (high = 70-100, medium = 30-70, and low = 0-30). The interviewer would ask the respondent to indicate the strength of his or her feelings by touching the appropriate level on the thermometer.[a]

The Communities: Physical and Social Environments

Located approximately one mile from the central city, the Core neighborhood is an area of transition, where census tracts are marked by a median age level of over 45, median family incomes ranging from $5,000 to $11,000 (in 1970), small apartment houses, residence hotels, and some older single-family dwellings and approximately 35 percent ethnic minority groups (1970). Slurb is a middle-class, predominantly white city, eight miles from downtown, on the edge of a middle-class black population, a median family income of $12,000, and an even distribution of single-family residences and apartment houses. Retirement is a relatively new, walled condominium and apartment community, with guarded entrances and a private security patrol. It is located 45 miles south of Los Angeles, adjacent to new regional shopping center, inhabited entirely by persons over 55 years of age, less than 2 percent being nonwhite, Spanish surname, and Asian, whose median family income was $11,000. The management corporation runs ads in one of the major metropolitan newspapers depicting, among other things, the security enjoyed by its residents, for example, a couple taking a walk at night. The three samples (although not their respective communities) are all white, 70 percent female, with ages ranging from 52 to 90.

Other characteristics relevant to fearful environments are socioeconomic levels, housing types, means of transportation, and perceived crime. Fifty-six percent of the Core group have an income of $4,000 or less and 81 percent live in apartments. Only 8 percent live in single-family residences. As for aspects of personal life that might be related to personal vulnerability, such as transportation, 50 percent are limited to walking or using a bus, and 65 percent are out of their homes for an average of five to eight hours per day.

Sixty-eight percent of the Slurb sample have an income of $4,000 or less and 54 percent live in single-family residences. Most likely these are persons who were middle income prior to retirement and are now remaining in their homes.

---

[a]This method was devised after a discussion with Stanley Turner who described similar approaches in fear of victimization studies.

In contrast to Core, the Slurb group is more mobile with only 22 percent limited to walking and/or the bus. Also, they are not out of their homes as much per day as the Core group.

Sixty-two percent of Retirement have an income of $10,000 or more and all but five of them live in condominiums with the remainder in apartments within the guarded walls. As for transportation all but 2 percent use or have access to an automobile. Also, a minibus service is provided free of charge so that residents can travel throughout the community and to an adjacent shopping center. Although the Retirement people go out of their home to a greater average number of places per day than the other two groups, they are away from their homes fewer average number of hours.

Finally, there is a difference the three groups in the level of dangerous crimes they perceive going on around them. In response to the question, "What kinds of crime occur in this community?" Forty percent of the Retirement residents said either there were none or named an offense not on the FBI index of serious crimes, compared with 32.1 percent of Slurb and 19.2 percent of Core.

Findings

Social Support

Gubrium (1974) suggests that supportive interpersonal relationships within age homogeneous areas should make a difference among elderly in the degree of anxiety about criminal victimization. Such environments for the elderly occur through a variety of ways and provide settings that may diffuse fear that when faced alone would be magnified and difficult to cope with. Using the number of persons living in the same residence, an estimate of the likelihood of neighbors calling the police if they saw the respondent being victimized, and the extent to which the person felt he or she was a part of the community as indicators of social support, the picture that emerges (see Table 5-1) is one of Core members being isolated individuals, with little apparent close social interaction, a low sense of dependence upon neighbors, and little solidarity with the community. In contrast, the Retirement group scored highest on all three of these indicators.

Perceived Safety

Another aspect of one's environment relative to the fear of crime is the perception of it as being safe or dangerous. Furstenburg (1971) suggests that the perception of safety in one's neighborhood is the basis for one's subjective definition of the risk of victimization.

Table 5-1
Mean Score Levels of Social Support Indicators

	Core (N = 26)	Slurb (N = 28)	Retirement (N = 50)
Number in residence	1.3[a]	1.6	1.7[b]
Likelihood of neighbors calling police	4.6[c]	6.6[d]	8.8[e]
Part of the community	4.1	5.3[f]	6.6[g]

[a]Level of significance, 2-tail test, between Core and Slurb < 0.5
[b]Level of significance, 2-tail test, between Core and Retirement < 0.01
[c]Level of significance, 2-tail test, between Core and Slurb < 0.05
[d]Level of significance, 2-tail test, between Slurb and Retirement < 0.001
[e]Level of significance, 2-tail test, between Core and Retirement < 0.001
[f]Level of significance, 2-tail test, between Slurb and Retirement < 0.10
[g]Level of significance, 2-tail test, between Core and Retirement < 0.01

The perception of safety was measured by asking how safe the person felt from crime in his immediate neighborhood during the day and night. Table 5-2 shows that (1) Retirement residents feel safer during the day than Core or Slurb, and Slurb feels slightly safer than Core; (2) all community groups feel safer during the day than night; (3) Retirement feels safer during the night than the other two; and (4) the greatest difference between feelings of safety at day and night are among the Core sample, then Slurb, and then Retirement. Thus, in similar order as the degree of social support, Retirement members perceive their neighborhood much safer than the other two and, consequently, perceive themselves to have a lower risk of victimization. In contrast, Core perceives themselves to have the greatest risk of victimization.

The Fear of Crime

The *fear of crime*, that is, the amount of anxiety and concern that persons have of being a victim, was measured by asking questions about specific crimes and situations. In terms of being a victim of four specific crimes—home burglarized, robbed on the streets, car stolen, and consumer fraud—the results as seen in Table 5-3 are consistently the same. For each crime, Core has the highest mean fear score, the lowest proportion indicating low fear, and the highest proportion indicating high fear. Not only are the mean scores ranked in the same order, but the differences between the means of Retirement and the other two groups are strikingly high. Also, three of the Core mean scores are higher than the highest score of Slurb, and all of the Slurb scores are higher than the Retirement scores; for example, even though Core ranks fraud as the lowest of their concerns, it is still higher than three of Slurb's concerns and all of Retirement fears.

Table 5-2
Mean Score Level of Perceived Safety From Victimization

	Core (N = 26)	Slurb (N = 28)	Retirement (N = 50)
Day	6.5[a]	7.0[b]	9.6
Night	3.2[c]	4.6[d]	9.0

[a]Level of significance, 2-tail test, between Core and Retirement < .001
[b]Level of significance, 2-tail test, between Slurb and Retirement < .001
[c]Level of significance, 2-tail test, between Core and Retirement < .001
[d]Level of significance, 2-tail test, between Slurb and Retirement < .001

Table 5-3
Mean Score Level of Fear of Victimization of Four Crimes

	Core (N = 26)	Slurb (N = 28)	Retirement (N = 50)
Home burglarized	4.9[a]	3.8[b]	0.6
Robbed on street	5.6[c]	4.7[d]	0.9
Car stolen	5.7[e]	3.6[f]	1.1[g]
Consumer fraud	4.3[h]	3.7[i]	1.9

[a]Level of significance, 2-tail test, between Core and Retirement < 0.001
[b]Level of significance, 2-tail test, between Slurb and Retirement < 0.001
[c]Level of significance, 2-tail test, between Core and Retirement < 0.001
[d]Level of significance, 2-tail test, between Slurb and Retirement < 0.001
[e]Level of significance, 2-tail test, between Core and Slurb $< 0.10; N = 10$
[f]Level of significance, 2-tail test, between Slurb and Retirement < 0.01
[g]Level of significance, 2-tail test, between Core and Retirement < 0.01
[h]Level of significance, 2-tail test, between Core and Retirement < 0.01
[i]Level of significance, 2-tail test, between Slurb and Retirement < 0.01

Besides comparing the samples' scores, one can also examine which incident the members of each community fear most and thereby gain further understanding of the areas of vulnerability felt by them. The highest levels of fear among the Core group were for auto theft and robbery on the street. For those members of the sample that have access to an automobile ($N = 10$) it is an extremely important element in providing mobility and security. Since most of the Core residents live in small, inexpensive apartment houses (presumably without garages), cars must be parked on the streets. As for being robbed on the streets, most of this sample is out on the streets for longer periods than the other groups, thus being vulnerable to street crime. Also, they perceive the streets as dangerous in that 49 percent listed robbery, aggravated assault, and other violent crimes as going on in the neighborhood.

For the Slurb residents, robbery on the streets receives the highest mean fear score. Similar to the Core group, they may tend to perceive their neighborhood environment as criminal and their home relative to the streets (see Rainwater 1966 re: home as haven) as secure. Also, as indicated by their low income, these groups may not have much of value in their homes, except television sets.

The mean level score for consumer fraud was the highest of four crimes among the Retirement residents and is an indication of wealth, combined with the real and perceived security of where they live. Although their concern about car theft (the second highest score) is another function of their economic status, it also reflects the perception that relatively more danger exists outside the community walls, such as in the parking lots of adjacent shopping centers or cultural and recreation centers in Los Angeles. One woman commented: "When I get off the freeway and through the gates, I always breath a sigh of relief." Because of the guarded entrances, the security patrols, and close proximity of neighbors, the level of fear of home burglary and street robbery within the community walls is practically negligible.

Since the questions of fear and safety dealt with the immediate community, another set of questions dealing with other situations or places that made them fearful was asked. All three of the samples had approximately the same percent saying that there were specific situations that made them fearful (Core—81%, Retirement—82%, and Slurb—86%). Generally, one could summarize the findings of other situations and places of fear by the following: Core appears to have a vague, generalized fear of many places and crimes, Slurb tends to feel most vulnerable to night time situations where one might be robbed or attacked, and Retirement tends to fear situations outside the walls of the community, where robbery or mugging may occur. Several of the responses among all three groups reflected anxiety in going to areas frequented by ethnic minority groups. Table 5-4 shows that all three had relatively high levels of fear of these situations, which indicates a sense of vulnerability and anxiety outside the home.

Security Precautions Taken

Besides attempting to document the existence the level of fear and concern about crime, another objective of the study was to examine how persons cope with an environment they perceive as dangerous or safe. Thus, a series of

Table 5-4
Mean Score Level of Amount of Fear in Other Specific Situations

	Core (N = 26)	Slurb (N = 28)	Retirement (N = 50)
Amount of fear in specific situations	6.2	7.6	7.0

questions was asked concerning precautions that had been taken out of a concern for security and protection from victimization by crime. The cautions included whether the person had obtained a weapon (including a gun), a watch dog, a whistle, or personal property and theft insurance, installed special locks on doors and/or windows, locks the door during the day while at home, participated in a police department property identification program, or changed any other behavior or activities. Table 5-5 provides the percentages of each sample that indicated that they have taken these precautions.

First, in comparing across the three samples, the Core group has the highest proportion in five of the eight measures, which are obtaining a weapon, obtaining a whistle, locking doors during the day, using the police property identification program, and changing behavior and attitudes. Of the three categories of behavior and attitude change, Core has the highest proportion state that they now stay home more. The Slurb group has the highest proportion to install locks on doors and windows and, among the changes in behavior, the highest proportion who expressed more cautious attitudes, for example, hide things, do not open the door at night. The Retirement group had the highest proportion who had property and theft insurance.

Looking at the rank order within each sample of the measures taken, the responses by Core residents indicate a priority placed on relatively low-cost

Table 5-5
Percentage of Three Samples Indicating Safety Precaution Taken for Security from Crime

	Core (N = 26)	Slurb (N = 28)	Retirement (N = 50)
Safety Precautions Taken:			
Obtain a weapon, including a gun	15.4	3.7	4.0
Obtain a watch dog	0.0	3.6	0.0
Obtain a whistle	42.3	25.0	0.0*
Install special locks	53.8	71.4	10.0*
Lock door during the day	96.0	89.3	38.0**
Obtain property theft insurance	16.0	33.3	47.9**
Police property identification	15.4	7.1	10.0
Change behavior and activities:	87.5	60.7	22.0**
Stay home	20.0	10.5	9.1
Stay home–night	65.0	47.4	54.5
More cautious	10.0	36.8	36.4
Hide things	5.0	5.3	0.0

*X^2 level of significance < 0.05.
**X^2 level of significance < 0.001.

precautions focused upon making the home a secure niche, for example, over half said they protect themselves by installing special locks, staying home, and locking the doors. The Slurb residents are similar in that the three largest categories are locking doors, installing special locks, and being more cautious. In contrast to the Core and Slurb groups, there was not one category of precaution that one half or more of the Retirement residents indicated that they took. Unlike the other two groups, it appears that they perceive their home as a secure environment and, thus, do not need to devote energies or resources for the provision of piecemeal security measures. As for the precautions many do take, the purchase of insurance against theft is a function of their wealth and serves as a standby measure only if the community security system fails and, even then, is a restoration of losses rather than a protection from loss. Also, the fact that over half of those who changed some behavior indicated they stay home at night suggests that some Retirement people may see the outside as dangerous.

The significance of these measures underscores the differences and paradoxes between the three samples in their life-styles. The Core group generally has fewer socioeconomic resources, a perception of a more criminal environment, a greater fear of crime, takes more precautions for security, and can count less on neighborhood support for security and protection, and the Retirement group has the greatest resources, a perception of noncriminal environment, the lowest fear of crime, takes the fewest security measures, and has the greatest sense of communal support.[b] This points up the need for providing appropriate formal means of control and protection for elderly in areas that do not have an insular character or creating informal networks to make up for the lack of resources. Also, it raises the question of how these groups feel toward the formal criminal justice agencies. Related to this, the members of each community were asked to evaluate the effectiveness of their local police in terms of carrying out their duties. Core residents ranked them lowest and Retirement gave the police

[b]Another difference between communities is housing type, with the Core and the Retirement groups living predominantly in apartments or condominiums and the Slurb group evenly balanced between apartments and single-family units. Although the size of the Slurb sample is too small ($N = 27$) to make broad generalizations, the differences obtained between housing type within the same community suggests a fruitful line of research.

First, as for social support, persons living in apartments are more likely to be living alone and less likely to expect neighbors to call the police in the event of crime being committed. There is no difference between the two subgroups' sense of being a part of the community. In terms of perception of safety, although a larger proportion of the single-family unit persons felt high safety during the day (86.7%) than apartment dwellers (58.3%), a larger proportion of apartment residents (33.3%) felt high safety during the evening (single unit = 13.3%). This suggests that even though persons living in single-family residences have greater social support than apartment dwellers, their feelings of safety diminish more abruptly as darkness comes than do apartment dwellers. This vulnerability is also seen in comparing the fear of home burglary and robbery on the street between the two groups. In contrast to no apartment dwellers indicating high fear of home burglary, 33.3% of the single units indicated high fear. As for robbery on the streets, although their level of fear is greater than for burglary, it is less than the fear felt by the single-unit group. These findings indicate the need for pursuing the question of type of housing and fear of victimization.

the highest evaluation, thus adding one more dimension to the picture of an alienated community.

Relationships within Communities

Although the differences between the samples are consistent throughout the analysis in supporting a typology of three environments related to fear of crime, there are differences between relationships within each sample that provide further information on the nature of their respective fearful environments. That is, how are a sense of social support, perception of safety, and the number of security precautions taken related to the fear of burglary, robbery, and consumer fraud within each community? (Auto theft was eliminated from this part of the analysis because of the low N in the Core sample's auto ownership.) Tables 5-6, 5-7, and 5-8 indicate the findings relevant to these questions, and the following statements are summaries of the findings:

1. Within Core, the relatively high negative associations between the fear of crime and two social support variables (the sense of being a part of one's community and relying on neighbors to call the police in the event of a crime being committed) suggest that social support and ties are the most important factors in diffusing the fear of having one's home burglarized, of being robbed on the streets, and, to a lesser extent, of being a victim of consumer fraud. (Alternative explanations to be investigated would be that fear of crime creates situations of distrust of others and, therefore, reduced indicators of support or

Table 5-6
Relationship between the Fear of Burglary and Social Support, Perceived Neighborhood Safety, and Number of Security Precautions in Three Communities

	Core (N = 26)	Slurb (N = 28)	Retirement (N = 50)
Support			
Number in residence	−0.14	0.10	0.18
Feel a part of the community	−0.61	−0.36	−0.06
Likelihood of neighbors calling the police	−0.47	−0.01	0.04
Safety			
Safety during the day	0.19	0.04	−0.34
Safety during the evening	0.11	−0.50	−0.65
Number of security precautions taken	0.30	0.15	−0.07

Note: Measure is Pearsonian *r*.

Table 5-7

Relationship between the Fear of Robbery and Social Support, Perceived Neighborhood Safety, and Number of Security Precautions in Three Communities

	Core (N = 26)	Slurb (N = 28)	Retirement (N = 50)
Support			
Number in residence	−0.06	−0.07	−0.03
Feel a part of the community	−0.35	−0.39	−0.24
Likelihood of neighbors calling the police	−0.39	−0.18	0.11
Safety			
Safety during the day	0.35	−0.12	−0.10
Safety during the evening	0.04	−0.59	−0.36
Number of security precautions taken	0.25	−0.10	0.05

Note: Measure is Pearsonian r.

Table 5-8

Relationship between the Fear of Consumer Fraud and Social Support, Perceived Neighborhood Safety, and Number of Security Precautions in Three Communities

	Core (N = 26)	Slurb (N = 28)	Retirement (N = 50)
Support			
Number in residence	0.001	0.27	0.16
Feel a part of the community	−0.23	−0.18	0.20
Likelihood of neighbors calling the police	−0.32	−0.02	−0.03
Safety			
Safety during the day	0.003	0.05	−0.20
Safety during the evening	0.12	0.08	−0.46
Number of security precautions taken	−0.25	−0.22	−0.09

Note: Measure is Pearsonian r.

that another variable, such as perception of a criminal environment, is causally linked to both.)

2. Among Retirement residents, the negative associations in the tables suggests that perceived safety from victimization in one's immediate neighborhood is most important in diffusing fear of the three types of crime. Further,

social support is less important than perceived safety in reducing fear in an area of high protectiveness, particularly in contrast to a central city area. (Again this assumes that fear of crime is a dependent variable.)

3. Comparing the associations among the Slurb residents, a feeling of belonging to the community and perceived safety of neighborhood at night contribute to a decrease in the level of fear of burglary and robbery, but not consumer fraud.

4. The associations between number of security precautions taken and fear of the three crimes are comparatively small for all three groups. For the Core group there is a positive association with fear of robbery and burglary, that is, the greater the number of precautions, the higher the level of fear of burglary and robbery. Thus, the number of precautions taken apparently does little in allaying fear of burglary or robbery. The exception is in the fear of consumer fraud where there are negative, although weak, relationships with the number of security precautions, that is, the higher the number of precautions, the lower the level of fear of fraud. It may be that in responding to the fear of numerous kinds of crime, the precautions taken provide a sense of protection or niche of security from deception, but not from personal or property crime and violence.

An issue here, similar to ones noted above that would require further theoretical and empirical investigation, is whether the precautions taken are indicators of the level of fear of crime or whether the level of fear increases as a result of taking security precaution. The latter case would be similar to a cycle where persons respond to their perception of a crime problem in the neighborhood by taking various precautions. In turn, the existence or use of these precautions function to heighten their sensitivity to the problem and, thereby, magnify their fears. Another possibility is that a third factor causes each.

5. As indicated by the low coefficients, the number of persons in one's residence does not appear to be as important as other factors in diffusing the fear of crime. Thus, in terms of Gubrium's hypothesis noted earlier, these findings indicate that living alone may not magnify the dangers of possible victimization as much as being socially isolated from neighbors and community groups. Further, there is some rather weak support for the speculation that living with others may increase one's sense of danger and anxiety about being burglarized at home or cheated in a consumer transaction among the Slurb and Retirement residents.

Policy Implications

In terms of policy implications of this study, the findings emphasize that fearful environments related to possible criminal victimization differ among elderly according to their living circumstances, which are primarily a function of dissimilarities in socioeconomic class and resources. Therefore, to be most effective, policy measures should reflect these differences. It is likely that the life circumstances of many low-income people regardless of age contribute to the factors underlying the fear of crime, for example, poor housing, inadequate public services, less community solidarity, and less power and political means to obtain services. Certainly the findings of this study suggest this for older persons. Thus, one option concerning the fear of crime would include broad and comprehensive social reform measures, such as better housing, increased social security benefits, greater income, that would seek to increase the social and economic resources and the quality of life of the low-income, urban elderly. (Such reform on a large scale throughout the age levels of society might also have the result of decreasing a large proportion of violent and property crime.)

As for more specific, less comprehensive measures, a variety of proposals have been made to reduce possible victimization or the anxiety and fear of it. Workshops and training programs dealing with self-defense, consumer protection, and residential security have mushroomed in numbers over the past few years. Furstenburg (1971, p. 609) notes the following possible measures: (1) requiring landlords to install protective devices in their apartment units;[c] (2) establishing "safe zones" in high crime areas where there would be security, supervised recreation, and transportation; and (3) providing victim insurance. This final section is devoted primarily to an analysis of a proposed safe niche in a fearful environment.

It appears that the safety felt by the Retirement group is a function of the highly secure and insular character of the community, which, in effect, is purchased along with other amenities when one buys a Retirement condominium; that is, there are some elderly who are able to buy protection from criminal victimization within their community. Their sense of vulnerability increases as they move outside of the walls of the community and especially to areas where large concentrations of minority groups are perceived. This vulnerability may even keep some members from going too far beyond the walls of the community. In a sense, the entire Retirement community serves as a secure niche for most of its residents.

For those elderly who live in less protected environments and who have less social support, fewer economic resources, and lower evaluation of the police, it appears they lack the sense of having a protective shield. Thus, they are more likely to turn to taking their own security measures in order to create small and private places of safety, such as their apartment unit or home. However, there are limitations to these remedies. They may not be an effective means of reducing fear and they tend to leave their users with a variety of geographic and temporal constraints. That is, these persons may not venture out of their protected havens during the evening and be hesitant to do so even during the

---

[c]The San Francisco Board of Supervisors has voted to require landlords to install burglar-resistant locks and windows in multiple-unit buildings by 1980 (*Los Angeles Times*, 1975b).

day. Therefore, policy measures that would provide for greater freedom within one's community ought to be proposed and analyzed.

Continuing Furstenburg's (1971) suggestion for safe zones, one could visualize the creation or further development of secure niches within neighborhoods that would provide a meeting place for elderly during the day or evening. Possibly these could be in already established centers for older persons, as in recreation centers, churches, or storefronts. Included in such a plan would be at least three essential components: (1) safe access, (2) secure facilities, and (3) meaningful activities and social participation. Implicit in all of these, as the following discussion will show, is an increased stake in the community to be realized by its members—an assumption that may not be realistic.

In order to insure safe access to and from such a niche, a much improved transportation system would need to be devised. As pointed out in the findings, the proportion of members of the Core community having an automobile was relatively low—one-half have to walk or use the bus (the latter being practically nonexistent in some areas of southern California at night). Some specific measures that would alleviate the sense of street vulnerability would be to institute free minibus or jitney service on a street by street or house-to-house basis. Improved lighting that would increase the public visibility of persons walking on sidewalks might also decrease the feeling of vulnerability at night. Finally, in order to enhance travel within one's neighborhood and, specifically, to and from the meeting place, community patrols could be established to oversee or insure safe transit. Such patrols might be made up of retired policemen or security guards, or, as Conklin (1975) describes, teenage gangs enlisted to support a community activity.

Besides safe access, there must be assurance that the meeting place is secure and free from violence or harassment. Similar to the street patrols, youthful or retired persons of the community could guard those places of the local environment designated to be secure. Also, there could be some means of identifying and limiting admittance to members only.

Along with safe access and secure facilities, there should be a variety of activities available for those who attend designed to, among other things (1) encourage a sense of participation and belonging in the life of the community, (2) provide a setting for friendships, trust, and mutual support, and (3) counsel with those who are particularly anxious about victimization. Such counsel could be in the form of (a) listening to and dealing with the expression of feelings about specific fearful circumstances, with the possible end result being neighborhood mobilization or a community action, such as obtaining better lighting or police protection, or (b) teaching crime prevention practices, such as consumer protection and antiburglary and robbery techniques.

Although specific programming and other measures would be a matter of peculiar needs and circumstances, for example, access to transportation, housing type, or other social or economic resources, the intended consequences of providing such niches of security in a community would be similar—to reduce the objective and subjective risks of victimization and to increase the sense of solidarity and mutual support among the residents. However, the possibility of unintended consequences requires some critical evaluation of such a proposal, too.

For example, what are the problems associated with the use of community patrol groups? Gary T. Marx and Dan Archer (1973, p. 47) point out that persons who tend to be attracted to modern vigilante or defense groups are "of uncertain temperaments" and tend to marginal community members. A second issue, concerning the legal power and means that such groups have in the assurance of neighborhood safety, is related to the complicated issue of security vs. individual rights. For example, crime-prevention programs that make use of police saturation of specific areas to reduce crimes are being questioned in terms of the constitutionality of their search and seizure practices (*Los Angeles Times* 1975a). To what extent are community patrols confronted with similar issues?

Besides the questions of membership and legality of community patrol groups to secure niches of safety in a community, the question of effectiveness should be raised. The findings from the Kansas City patrol experiment—that variation in the differences in the level of preventive patrol by police makes no difference in the amount of victimization or the level of fear of crime (Kelling et al. 1974)—have implications for the use and success of community patrols.

Another unanswered question posed by such a measure—and likely in other crime prevention programs—is whether one of the consequences would be an intensification of anxiety about victimization. Although not denying the reality of crime, especially in an urban area where the elderly reside, to what extent do programs intended to increase protection and safety also function to sensitize them to the problem to the point they are more frightened? The greater the degree of fright they feel, the less likely they will be to venture out into the community, which, in turn, intensifies their fear of crime.

A final policy question to be raised is whether it is possible to establish a safe place without creating the aura of an exclusive fortress separated from the rest of the community. To some observers, Retirement appears to be a secure niche that has been purchased by its residents at the additional cost of isolation from the larger community. To what extent is this true? To what extent is it desirable?

This final section has presented some measures that might attack the problem of fearful environments experienced by urban elderly. However, it has also posed questions about the measures proposed and, by implication, other means of reducing the fear of victimization. The intent was not to cover every possible objection to the establishment of niches of safety nor to deny the reality of such environments, but rather to analyze them in terms of whether they are legal, appropriate, and effective. All of these are researchable questions that ought to be pursued, the answers to which should be included in the public debate.

References

Block, Richard L. 1971. "The fear of crime and fear of police." *Social Problems* 19 (Summer): 91-101.

Boggs, Sarah L. 1971. "Formal and informal crime control: An exploratory study of urban, suburban, and rural orientations." *Sociological Quarterly* 12 (Summer): 1-9.

Conklin, John E. 1971. "Dimensions of community response to the crime problem." *Social Problems* 18 (Winter): 373-85.

_____ . 1975. *The Impact of Crime.* New York: Macmillan.

Ennis, Philip H. 1967. *Criminal Victimization in the United States: A Report of a National Survey.* Washington, D.C.: President's Commission on Law Enforcement and Administration of Justice, Field Surveys II.

Furstenburg, Frank. 1971. "Public reactions to crime in the streets." *American Scholar* (Autumn): 601-10.

Gubrium, Jaber, 1974. "Victimization and three hypotheses." *Crime and Delinquency* 20 (July): 245-50.

Kelling, George, T. Pate, D. Dieckman, and C.E. Brown. 1974. *The Kansas City Preventive Patrol Experiment: A Summary Report.* Washington, D.C.: Police Foundation.

Los Angeles Times. 1973. "Survey lists concerns of retirants." April 5, 1973.

_____ . 1975a. "Pasadena: Rights vs. Security." May 25, 1975.

_____ . 1975b. "Burglar-Resistant Locks in Multi-Unit Buildings Required." May 29, 1975.

Marx, Gary T., and Dan Archer. 1973. "The urban vigillante." *Psychology Today* (January): 45-50.

McIntyre, J. 1967. "Public attitudes toward crime and law enforcement." *The Annals* 374 (November): 34-46.

Rainwater, Lee. 1966. "Fear and the house-as-haven in the lower class." *Journal of the American Institute of Planners* 32 (January): 23-33.

Savitz, Leonard. 1972. "Intergenerational patterns of the fear of crime." Paper presented at the InterAmerican Congress on Criminology, Caracas, Venezuela, November 19-25.

Patterns of Age Integration in Public Housing and the Incidence and Fears of Crime among Elderly Tenants

Edmund A. Sherman,
Evelyn S. Newman,
and *Anne D. Nelson*

The Problem: Age-Integrated versus Age-Segregated Housing

Public housing policy for the elderly must take many factors into consideration. Professional gerontologists have long held that *age-integrated neighborhoods* (that is, neighborhoods in which elderly people are living side-by-side with younger families) are better for elderly people than age-segregated neighborhoods. They assume that different age groups in normal neighborhoods will develop needed social intercourse and mutual support.[a]

Many criminal justice experts, on the other hand, concerned about the victimization of the aged by crime and their demoralization by fears of crime, advocate age-segregated housing for the elderly. They maintain that crimes against the aged in public housing can be nearly eliminated if buildings are exclusively designed and reserved for the elderly.[b] In addition, social welfare experts have noted that service delivery to the elderly is considerably enhanced where client groups are concentrated, as in age-segregated housing situations. The recurrent problems of transportation and access to age-relevant needs of the elderly are effectively overcome in such living arrangements.[c]

This study was funded by a grant from the Institute for Public Policy Alternatives, State University of New York. This chapter has also been published under the title "Living Arrangements and Security among the Elderly in Public Housing," *HUD Challenge*, June 1976.

[a]Irving Rosow has stated the gerontological position: "They (gerontologists) dislike segregated and isolated patterns because they seem undemocratic, invidious and demoralizing. They like age integration particularly for the alienated with disrupted lives. They assume that different age groups in normal neighborhoods will develop social intercourse and mutual support. More formally stated, they believe that residential integration will maximize social integration. This is the critical premise." Irving Rosow, "Retirement Housing and Social Integration," in Clark Tibbits and Wilma Donahue (eds.), *Social and Psychological Aspects of Aging* (N.Y.: Columbia University Press, 1962), p. 329.

[b]The perspective of the criminal justice community has been outlined by John Edie: "(H)ousing that is exclusively designed, exclusively reserved for the elderly will cut out the crime in the building 100 percent. . . . The major problem we have run across in all the examples I have given you today have dealt with housing projects where the elderly have mixed in with families and there has just been no way of control. What happens essentially is that a great deal of the crime that is committed against the elderly is committed by people who live right in the project and if they live in your building it's pretty hard to keep them out." John Edie, "Keynote Talk," in Noel E. Tomas, *Reducing Crimes Against Aged Persons*, Federal Regional Council Task Force Workshop Report (Philadelphia: 1974), p. 8.

[c]Gelwicks and Newcomer recommend "such programs as the development of multiservice, community senior centers on the same site as the housing." Louis E. Gelwicks and Robert J. Newcomer, *Planning Housing Environments for the Elderly* (Washington, D.C.: National Council on the Aging, Inc., 1974), p. 4.

In order to determine which of these two positions is better policy for elderly residents of public housing, the Institute of Gerontology, a part of the School of Social Welfare at State University of New York at Albany conducted a survey of elderly residents in different types of public housing in the Albany-Troy area. The purpose of the study was to explore the effects of different living arrangements on the numbers and kinds of crimes involving elderly victims, to determine the fears and attitudes of the residents concerning their personal safety, and to assess past and present attempts to insure their safety.

Methods: The Interviews

A major facet of the study was an interview survey of tenants of three types of public housing arrangements for the elderly in the Albany-Troy area. The three types consisted of age-integrated, age-segregated, and a mixed arrangement of age-segregated units within an age-integrated project.

Two projects in the city of Albany were selected to represent the age-integrated pattern of housing. Initially, the John Boyd Thacher Homes was selected, but when this study began in July 1974, elderly residents of the Thacher Homes were being moved out to other projects as a result of a policy decision made by the Albany Housing Authority. (The factors in this decision were complex and beyond the scope of this project.) Consequently, only four residents were interviewed from that setting. The other age-integrated setting was the Lincoln Park Homes, which consists of 275 units in which elderly tenants occupy about 110 units and live side-by-side with families of different ages. A total of 60 interviews were obtained in this setting, and because of this the preponderance of data in this study concerning age-integrated housing is based on the responses of Lincoln Park residents.

The age-segregated setting of the study was Kennedy Tower, a single high-rise building in Troy, New York, with 266 units occupied entirely by elderly families and individuals. Finally, the mixed housing pattern was represented by Ida Yarbrough Homes, an Albany project consisting of two high-rise buildings of 112 units each. These buildings, situated in the midst of low-rise buildings that house younger adults and their families, are limited strictly to elderly residents.

The selection of residents for interviews within these settings was in the nature of a purposive sample. A list of elderly residents was obtained from the housing management in each project, and the persons selected from the list were contacted by letter or telephone to request their participation in an interview. Our intent was to interview a minimum of 50 respondents in each type of setting so as to be able to meaningfully calculate percentages and make comparisons among the types of settings in terms of descriptive statistics. Since this was not a probability sample, inferential statistics were not used in the analysis of the data.

A total of 169 interviews was obtained: 64 in age-integrated housing, 55 from the age-segregated setting, and 50 from the mixed setting. The interviews were conducted either by the research project staff or by paid graduate students from the School of Social Welfare at SUNY Albany. A 14-page interview schedule, which was pretested on a small sample of elderly residents, was used for the survey. The majority of questions in the schedule were structured, with a few open-ended ones for more exploratory items.[d]

Even though word of the coming of our interviewers had been spread throughout the buildings by management and each of our interviewers carried identification, there were some respondents who were so fearful they would admit no strangers into their apartments. Initially, there were 15 refusals of in-person interviews in the age-integrated setting. We attempted to compensate for this by obtaining some interviews by telephone rather than face to face.[e] Eleven interviews were obtained in this manner, thereby leaving only 4 outright refusals in that setting. There were 3 refusals in the age-segregated setting. This is a total of 7 refusals relative to 169 completed interviews, for a refusal rate of about 4 percent.

A second major facet of the study was a survey of project managers, public housing officials, security personnel, and police officials concerning security practices and problems in the study settings. Consultants to this project from the faculty of the School of Criminal Justice at SUNYA met with the project staff to determine the content areas to be explored and the officials to be surveyed in this aspect of the study. An interview schedule consisting of general, open-ended questions of an exploratory and descriptive nature was drafted, and the survey was carried out by one of the project staff members who was also a doctoral candidate in criminal justice.[f] He conducted interviews with a total of 15 officials on various aspects of public housing security and measures designed to protect the elderly. In addition, demographic data based on census tracts and data on crime frequency were obtained on the projects for which such data were available, as well as crime incidence data for the respective neighborhoods.

The data from the survey of tenants were coded and punched on IBM cards for processing by computer. The major focus of the resulting statistical analysis was to cross-tabulate each relevant variable by type of housing pattern, that is,

[d]Originally, questions were compiled from Philip H. Ennis, *Criminal Victimization in the United States*, NORCO, May 1967, and the U.S. Department of Justice, LEAA, *Crimes and Victims: A Report on the Dayton-San Jose Pilot Survey of Victimization* (Washington, D.C.: June 1974). On the basis of consultations with the two faculty members from criminal justice and since we wanted an interview that would last no more than 45 minutes, our final 14-page schedule was developed.

[e]One respondent reported keeping a can of bug spray next to her door for protection in the event that someone unwanted should attempt to enter. She insisted that she trusts no one. The interviewer was unable to gain access to the apartment and the interview was conducted over the telephone.

[f]See Chapter 15.

age-segregated, age-integrated, and mixed. In this way frequencies on each variable could be compared for differences and similarities among the three housing arrangements. In addition, cross-tabulations of other variables were carried out to control or look for possible interactive effects.

Results: The Findings of the Survey

This section of the report includes only the highlights and salient findings of the tenant survey.

Beginning with the actual incidence of crime against elderly tenants, it was found that there were markedly more respondents in age-integrated housing who reported that they had been victims of crime. Table 6-1 shows the clear differences by type of housing.

Of the 25 victims in the age-integrated setting, 4 had been victims of robbery, 5 of larceny (purse snatching), 2 of assault and 8 of burglary. Five respondents had been victims of nonclassified crimes[g] and 1 respondent reported a crime but refused to give further information.

Of the 7 victims from the mixed setting, (some of these crimes had occurred at a previous address), 2 had been victims of robbery, 2 of larceny, and 3 of burglary. Of the 8 victims in the age-segregated setting, 5 had been victims of larceny, 1 of assault, and 2 nonclassified.

Three people in the age-integrated and 2 in the age-segregated settings were victims of a crime more than once while living in their respective projects. (One unfortunate respondent had been victimized on 4 different occasions. Four times her purse had been stolen—twice in the elevator of her building and twice when she was outside the building.) Also, a higher percentage of respondents in the age-integrated housing were aware of other tenants in their buildings having been victimized than was true in the other two types of housing. Further, the

Table 6-1
Percentage of Respondents Who Reported Having Been Victims of Crime

| Tenant Victims of Crime | Type of Housing | | | |
	Mixed (N = 50) Percent	Age Integrated (N = 64) Percent	Age Segregated (N = 55) Percent	Total (N = 69) Percent
Yes	2.0	37.5	14.5	19.5
No	86.0	60.9	85.5	76.3
At other residence	12.0	1.6	0	4.1
Total	100.0	100.0	100.0	100.0

[g]The nonclassified crimes included vandalism and harassment.

majority of the crimes in the age-integrated setting occurred in the building, 11 inside the apartments, 5 elsewhere in the building, and 5 in the elevator. In the age-segregated building, on the other hand, only 2 of the 8 crimes occurred in the apartment whereas 4 occurred on the grounds, 1 on the neighborhood streets and 1 elsewhere.

The majority of crimes happened in the daytime (60%). In the age-integrated setting most crimes occurred in the apartments, elevators, or somewhere else in the building. In the age-segregated setting most crimes occurred in the apartment or grounds.

The differences between the types of housing in terms of fears of crime is even more dramatic than the differences in the actual incidence of crime. Thus, the evidence is quite clear with respect to incidence and fear of crime that age-integrated buildings are the least preferred. It should be noted that the "mixed" type of housing in this study is in fact age-segregated by building, so that it can be said that segregated buildings show more positive results from a security and morale standpoint. See Table 6-2.

Another interesting finding that has implications for public housing policy is the discrepancy between feelings of safety in the building by type of housing and feelings of safety in the neighborhood. The tenants in the age-segregated project showed a somewhat higher degree of fear of crime in their neighborhood than did tenants in the other two types of project. However, in spite of this fearfulness of the neighborhood not one of them, nor one from the mixed setting, indicated that he or she wanted to move from current housing because of fears of crime, whereas 42 percent of the respondents from the age-integrated setting said they wished to move. This was further evidence of the more secure feelings of residents of age-segregated buildings.

The respondents primary recommendation for better security in all types of settings was to hire more and better guards.[h] This recommendation was far greater in frequency than any other safety measure (suggested by them), for example, locking doors, tenant selection, etc. When respondents were asked what they thought of having tenants patrol the building most did not like the idea.[i]

---

[h]This response by the tenants appears to be in agreement with Lawton's recommendation for additional security: "In public housing there has been a constant question of the responsibility of local police as compared to housing authority security personnel. Many authorities have considered it impossible to spend money to hire their own security people, yet have been unable to exact adequate production from local police. We cannot advise clearly one way or another on this issue, except to urge every authority to stretch its budget to the very limit in the matter of personal security. Even with reasonably good local police protection, supplementary private service can add something extra to the general feeling of ease." M. Powell Lawton, *Planning and Managing Housing for the Elderly* (N.Y.: John Wiley and Sons, 1975), p. 137.

[i]A major reason for the dislike of having tenants act as patrol is that they are not in the position of being able to keep each other's children under control without causing hard feelings.

Table 6-2
Respondents' Feelings of Safety in Building during the Day

Feelings of Safety	Type of Housing			
	Mixed (N = 50) Percent	Age Integrated (N = 54) Percent	Age Segregated (N = 55) Percent	Total (N = 169) Percent
Very safe	82.0	29.7	92.7	65.7
Somewhat safe	16.0	37.5	3.6	20.1
Somewhat fearful	2.0	26.6	1.8	11.2
Very fearful	0.0	4.7	0.0	1.8
No information	0.0	1.6	1.8	1.2
Total	100.0	100.0	100.0	100.0

This finding tended to dovetail with findings from the security survey. Most of the security staff in the study settings were also tenants, and they felt a role conflict, which made for poor morale on their part and little confidence in them on the part of the tenants.

Other findings of interest from the security survey indicated that security practices and staffing tended to follow the age patterns of the buildings. In the age-integrated housing the paid security staff were more numerous, more formally organized, and more active with regard to patrolling of the premises. In the age-segregated and mixed housing, on the other hand, security tended to be more passive or less patrol oriented, with more informal security activities on the part of the tenants themselves, and a major reliance on monitoring the main entrance. One other safety feature of the age-segregated and mixed settings that differed from the age-integrated was that each room was equipped with an emergency alarm button, which simultaneously rings an alarm and lights up a panel in the front office identifying the apartment.

Implications of the Findings: Type of Housing and
Security Arrangements

The findings of this study tend to support the concept of age-segregated public housing for the aged as a means of reducing the incidence and fear of crime among this vulnerable sector of our population. Tenants in age-segregated buildings feel secure in their buildings even while feeling anxious in the neighborhood.[j] It seems that most public housing developments tend to be built

[j]Several respondents from the age-integrated buildings reported that in addition to feeling insecure and fearful in the neighborhood they had the same fears in their buildings. It was only behind the locked doors of their apartments they had any feelings of safety.

in urban areas with low land values, high crime, and the least desirable locations from a commercial point of view. If this is truly dictated by economic necessity, the implications for public policy become apparent. It behooves us to plan at least for more secure, age-segregated buildings.

From our analysis, therefore, the development of age-segregated housing for the elderly appears to be the first priority. This seems to offer not only a more secure environment but also one more capable of filling the social need of companionship. In age-segregated buildings, fears may be reduced still further through the services of a paid security guard but this appears to have a more limited effect on the fears of elderly residents of age-integrated buildings. As a second priority, however, the services of a trained, commensurately paid, security staff may offer further advantages. Finally, it was found in the course of this survey that residents generally have little or no input into security arrangements. Some form of liaison between tenant associations and security personnel may, therefore, bring forth a more mutually supportive framework for dealing with the problem of security.

Policy Alternatives

Based on the implications of our findings, and with the primary objective of reducing crime and fear of crime among the elderly, we are making the following policy recommendations:

1. First priority in future planning for public housing for the elderly should be given to age-segregated projects.
2. Where age-segregated *projects* are not feasible, economically or otherwise, certain *buildings* should at least be set aside exclusively for the aged within projects.
3. Since the tenants' major recommendation for enhancing security was to have additional and more competent security guards, it is proposed as a second priority that better trained and paid security personnel should be provided for in future budgetary considerations.
4. In line with number 3 above, we recommend discontinuance of current New York State policy against the use of funds for hiring and maintenance of security staff in state-funded public housing.
5. We recommend that periodic instruction in safety and security for public housing tenants be developed by local police. Respondents in this study who received such instruction attested to its helpfulness.
6. We also recommend increased usage of electronic safety devices, not only as an adjunct to the security forces, but to enhance the natural surveillance capacity of the tenants themselves. The alarm warning bell system in two of our settings highly was valued by residents for both security and mutual emergency aid generally.

**Part II
Criminal Victimization
of the Elderly**

7

Aging as Victimization: Reflections on the American Way of (Ending) Life

Jeffrey H. Reiman

We live in a time when the number of elderly people is vastly increasing as a result of a wide variety of medical advances unknown to prior generations. We also live in a time when the particular vulnerabilities of the aged are increasingly brought home to us as reports of inadequate health care, pension frauds, and Kafkaesque retirement homes fill the news media. Perhaps nothing, however, reveals both the unique vulnerability of the aged and the peculiar ambivalence of the young as much as the problem of crimes against the elderly. Such acts enrage us but they fail to galvanize us into action. We pity the old, but scarcely protect them. We hold their attackers in contempt, but only lightly punish them.

Many respond to this problem with proposals for increased police protection and more adequate security services tailored to the special infirmities of the aged. This is of course all to the good, and it should be supported by all—if not for moral reasons then out of prudential concern for their own eventual fate. But, such approaches miss the real source of the problem since they seek mainly to protect the aged against a small minority of vicious attackers. The problem is both deeper and wider. The old have to be protected against all of us. Crimes against the elderly are merely the most visible aspect of a process of victimizing the aged in which virtually all of us share. To focus simply on crimes against the elderly is to abdicate our own responsibility for creating and tolerating a situation in which the aged are viewed as less valuable than the young, a situation in which too many people are tempted to commit crimes against the elderly because they have also come to believe that the larger society does not really care.

Victimization of the aged cannot be fully understood unless it is seen in a larger social context in which *aging itself has been rendered a process of victimization*. We have created and we sustain (in a variety of ways) a society in which becoming old is not merely becoming different: Becoming old is moving away from optimal human characteristics; becoming old is becoming less human or more dead. So, when the process ends in physical death it appears as the culmination of a dying that started at the close of middle age and is indeed sometimes greeted by those still living with a sigh of relief as if the death has put the survivors out of their misery—the ambiguous misery of waiting for the living dead to become the dead dead.

There is undoubtedly a sense in which becoming old is becoming less of something. The aging person becomes less strong, less quick, less smooth of skin or sure of step. Perhaps the aging person becomes less sharp mentally or less flexible in his beliefs, although there is plenty of evidence that senility is created by the society that denies old people opportunity to exercise their wits, and it is surely our conceit to believe that rigidity is the monopoly of the old. It is of course a commonplace to observe that becoming less in these ways is no more objectively becoming less human than losing weight is. It is rather our collective value judgment—a judgment built into our institutions and media—that erects the qualities of youth as the optimal qualities of being human so that becoming old is equated with becoming less human.

To reject this view—and reject it we must when once we have seen an aging man or woman in the vain and undignified struggle not to be what he or she is ineluctably becoming—we do not have to go so far as to deny that attributes like strength and mental perspicacity are objectively important human characteristics. They are important, and their loss constitutes a real diminution in certain human capacities. What is necessary, however, is to note that the diminution in certain human capacities is not a diminution in humanity and, second, that there are other ways in which becoming old is clearly becoming more of something. It sounds trite to say that old people become more wise, and certainly there is something antique about this claim. Nevertheless if we think of wisdom not as the accumulated sediment of human knowledge but rather as the kind of knowledge about life that only comes when one can look at a period of 20 or 30 years as a passing phase rather than as an endless present, there is a sense in which becoming old means becoming more possessed of that rich understanding that sees the transcience of what the young person sees as permanent. Such a knowledge—aware as it is of the predictable ways in which human institutions change unpredictably—is likely to be both more skeptical and more charitable, less self-righteous, and self-satisfied than the quickly learned and quickly revised understanding of the young or moderately experienced. To be able to look at life as stretching over three or four generations, to see a marriage or a life's work, indeed to see adulthood itself with its eternal scrambling, as phases through which one passes, is to bring to experience a uniquely rich perspective for which we are wholly dependent upon the aged.

But becoming old can be becoming more in other ways. With a life satisfactorily lived mostly behind one, an individual can be more stable and less competitive, more tolerant and less judgmental, less in need to prove his worth. Such a person might be expected to be more able to rest with dignity on finite but real accomplishments rather than to derive uncertain glory from the sound and fury of the unlimited potential and seemingly unlimited energy of those whose lives are still to be made.

Finally, to say something that sounds most subjective but that really is most objective: to become old is to become more beautiful when beauty no longer trades on the unearned profits of young tissue, but rather when beauty in human beings is the incarnation of character tried and proven over the years.

All of this is not intended as a sentimental paean to old age; it is meant simply to flesh out the claim that although we live in a society in which becoming old is becoming less, this is not a necessary response to the physiological process of aging. Objectively, aging is becoming less in some ways and more in others. It is against this background we can see a society that defines aging as becoming less of a human being is guilty of a victimization of the old, which is built into the social meaning of aging itself.

The link between the victimization we have built into aging and the victimization of the aged by criminals is perhaps not readily apparent. My argument rests on several assumptions about American social attitudes: I assume we are an extremely decent and generous people who have nevertheless determined that some groups of people are "legitimate victims." When a group is labeled a "legitimate victim" we convey the subtle message that the members victimization is not as terrible as that of "normal" folks, that we will not respond to their victimizers with the outrage and vindictiveness reserved for the victimizers of the normals. We are more outraged when white students are shot than when black students are, but in neither case are we as outraged as when a white businessman is kidnaped and held for ransom. We are moved to sympathy and charity when Asians are victims of a natural disaster but not to indignation when they are murdered at close range or at a distance. We are prone to believe that women who are raped or blacks or hippies who are brutalized got what they deserved at least in part. In each of these cases, without so much as saying so explicitly, the green light is given to the would-be victimizers of a given group of people. My point is that in rendering aging itself a process of victimization we have given the green light to those who would assault and plunder the old.

To become old in America is to become substandard, defective as a human being. To be defective as a human being is to be in need of help, to exist by the charity of the young and the normal. By a curious alchemy, catalyzed perhaps by American fear of dependency, to be "in need of help" metamorphoses into "being a burden" or "not carrying one's own weight," which becomes "taking advantage," "taking more than one contributes," "being more trouble than one is worth." In other words to be in need of help in America is to be an object of scorn. To receive charity is to be denied respect. To be denied respect means that one is not immediately identified with as someone just like us, which means in turn that one's suffering is weighted less—all of which amounts to being labeled a legitimate victim, someone who can be harmed without exciting the normal sympathetic responses and collective outrage. By a form of the same chemistry that creates legitimate victims of poor people and dissenters, of blacks and women, we transform the old into legitimate victims by the victimization built into the process by which they move into the identity that society holds for them.

Let us look briefly at the processes that work in our society to convert the old into the needy and the scorned.

I have already remarked that to be young is to live very much with one's future as a source of the meaning of one's life. Growing old means living in the face of a shrinking future. The old person can no longer define himself in terms of the peaks to be scaled, the fame to be achieved, the skill to be mastered. What he is already is very much what he can hope to become. This means that the aged must find a sense of their worth and must convey to society a sense of the value of their contribution, in their present works and past accomplishments.

But we live in a society that has dived headlong into rapid social and technological change. As a result we have little respect for the skills and knowledge that take a lifetime to develop, so we offer the old few meaningful opportunities to display their unique abilities in situations tailored to their altered physical condition. The old are put out to pasture. The old are forced into retirement and idleness at arbitrarily selected ages, which often bear no real connection to their capacity for efficient work. Sometimes overnight, a respected and self-respecting worker becomes a bored idler with nothing but time on his hands to experience the self-doubt that accompanies the separation from productive work in a society like ours. Like muscles unused, minds unchallenged atrophy and become dull, "proving" by a through-the-looking-glass logic the appropriateness of forcing the old to retire in the first place. In a society like ours where the question "What do you do?" is answered by giving one's occupation, retirement is withdrawal not merely from work but from life itself.

But more than this the process of rapid change undermines the solidity of past accomplishments. In an earlier time, not only were the aged respected for their wisdom, but they lived out their lives in the stable surroundings of the village in which they were born. The village bore physical as well as human testimony to the accomplishments of a lifetime. Such conditions still obtain for the rural old, but increasingly an old person now is likely to be living in a town other than his birthplace, perhaps other than the place of his adulthood. He is almost certainly living in a building that did not exist when he was young. But what undoubtedly undermines the stability of his past the most is the fact that he is likely to spend his old age in the company of people he has only recently met, or perhaps with whom he has been arbitrarily thrown together to die in a nursing home.

There can be no doubt that people derive strength and meaning from the communities in which they exist. But community is more than a batch of people in proximity. It is not constituted merely by a common fate, or else ghettos or prisons or hospitals or concentration camps would automatically be communities—which they are not. Community is constituted by experiences shared over the years or by common purpose. An example of the former is the community that characterizes those who have spent their lives together in a village or a neighborhood; an example of the latter is the community of those who share similar political or professional goals. Increasingly the old are deprived of the former and excluded from the latter. True community may emerge from placing the aged together, but by no means automatically.

Surely there can be nothing more frightening and disheartening even to a young person than knowing he will die in the midst of people he has not yet met and with whom all he shares is the imminence of death. So, not only is the aged person put out to pasture, but out to strange pasture, to fields that hold no memories, to die in the midst of others who know his life only second hand. Deprived of a future by nature and of present and past by society, both he and we are deprived of a sense of his worth. His life as a source of value truly ends before his physical death. In the interim he is a burden, living only by our help, not contributing anything, an object of our disdain and our scorn.

The old are dispensable because we have already dispensed with them. From this root springs self-fulfilling prophecies like so many branches. The old are senescent so they cannot do productive challenging work or occupy respected roles in the community. So, they must do make-work or nothing and be thrust into artificial communities of other old people not of their kin or choice, and their capacities atrophy and they become senescent. Old people are weak and dying. So, it is useless to devote too much of our limited resources to their health and nutrition, and they become weak and die. But as a result of all these the most deadly prophecy fulfills itself. Rendered weak and sickly and deprived of opportunity to display their contributions to the community, our contribution to their support seems unrequited. It is not a payment for a valuable service rendered, but our charity. In other words, given no chance to be anything but a burden they become no more than burdens. As mere burdens we may owe them kindness but not respect. Deprived of the real effective respect that would be evidenced by outrage at their suffering and readiness to come to their defense, they are ready targets for victimization with impunity.

8 Crimes, Victims, and Justice

Emilio C. Viano

The Development of Victimology

Criminology, as a field of study, is a recently developed discipline, having been in existence for about a century, and is still a growing one. While scholars from the human behavior sciences group were developing theories about human behavior in general, criminologists focused on criminal behavior. Thus, for the early criminologists the main subject of study was the criminal. However, in recent years, the focus has shifted to the crime itself, not only as a legal entity, but as a complex situation reflecting the interaction between different actors and the cultural norms and expectations of society, and as the product of the intricate interplay of emotional, rational, incidental, and situational factors.

Consequently, attention and interest have developed about the victim as an integral part of the criminal situation. Scholars have begun to see the victim not necessarily just as a passive object, as the neuter or innocent point of impact of crime into society, but as eventually playing an active role or possibly contributing in different measure to his own victimization. During the last 30 years, there has been a spur of speculation, debate, and research on the victim, his role, the criminal-victim relationship, the concept of responsibility, the crime motive, and on behaviors that could be considered provocative. At the same time, certain types of criminal behavior have been identified as being victimless.

Thus, the study of crime has acquired a more realistic and complete outlook. Criminologists have recognized the different elements that constitute a crime, and they study them within their dynamic context, attempting to understand their interrelationship and therefore detect explanatory patterns.

Much of the preliminary study of crime from this comprehensive point of view has been of an inventory-taking nature. This is of course a basic prerequisite for the development of systematic typologies and theories.

Although the founders of criminology were themselves aware of the crucial importance of the criminal-victim relationship, it was not until the 1940s that a high level interest in the victim developed. Hans von Hentig's paper entitled "Remarks on the Interaction of Perpetrator and Victim" (1940) and his book, *The Criminal and His Victim* (1948); Mendelsohn's paper "New Bio-psychosocial Horizons: Victimology" (1956); and Ellenberger's study on the psychological relationship between the criminal and his victim (1954) all underlined the importance of studying the criminal-victim relationship in order to obtain a better understanding of crime, and of its origins and implications. Since then

83

numerous scholars have focused their efforts on this aspect of the criminal situation. As a result, a considerable body of literature on the victim has been developed.

Meanwhile, a movement for the recognition of the victim as deserving more effective remedy than the traditional action in tort was begun by the late English Penal Reformer Margery Fry (1951). Her call for reform was first heard in New Zealand in 1963. In that year, the New Zealand Parliament established the first crime compensation tribunal, with discretionary power to award public compensation to the victim or his dependents where he had been injured or killed through the commission of certain specified offenses. In the following year, the Tory government in England announced a similar, but nonstatutory program. In America, the first jurisdiction to adopt the compensation principle was California. Its program was enacted in 1965 and put in operation two years later. Since that time, similar or related programs have been established in New York (1966), Hawaii (1967), New Jersey (1971), and several other states. Today, many propose a different and further step to provide for the compensation of persons injured by certain criminal acts—an insurance system.

The interest of scholars and professionals on victims and their relationship with their criminals has reached now a significant momentum. International recognition that victimology is indeed a vital branch of the study of crime has been given at the First International Symposium on Victimology held in Jerusalem in September 1973 and at the International Institute on Victimology (Bellagio, Italy, 1975).

New Perspectives Opened by Victimological Research

Three varieties of interest are recognizable in the work of the growing number of students of victimology:

1. Scientific, that is, a principal interest in the causal association of victim and offender acts and characteristics.
2. Social engineering, reflected by those concerned directly with measures to reduce the hazards of victimization, including efforts to increase the chances of offender detection and prosecution.
3. Legal and moral, displayed by those concerned with more accurate and just assignments of responsibility, blame, fault, guilt, culpability, mitigation, etc. Some of these measures entail fundamental alterations of systems of law and the administration of justice.

Research focusing on the victim has brought new perspectives into the social sciences:

1. Students of crime who focus on the individual and his characteristics

have a new set of research targets. In the past, the offender has been almost exclusively at the center of interest. Much effort has been spent in attempting to find out what peculiarities, anomalies, mental disorders, personality defects, could explain criminal behavior. Now the same types of questions are raised about the victim. Many talk about victim proneness, victim recidivists, victim in need, latent victim, etc. This obviously implies that there may be something in those who are victimized, particularly in those who are repeatedly victimized, that may explain their victimization.

2. Victim-focused research and interest has somewhat redressed the balance in crime-related research. In the past, society has been much more preoccupied to assign the offender a certain societal role and to keep him in it. This labeling of the offender has been accomplished by describing him as a different kind of person, evil, sick, mentally deranged, or as an outsider, and an outcast. The victim has also been seen and described as an innocent party whose unlucky fate it was to fall victim to a violent crime. Victimology, by introducing a new perspective, has contributed to the softening or elimination of these stereotypes. One could almost say the balance has already swung too far in the other direction, and for a good reason: a new scapegoat has been found to explain criminal behavior, the victim. Some criminologists, or would-be ones, have quickly seized the opportunity to claim that victims of assault have no one else but themselves to blame if they were attacked when walking, let us say, in a dark alley; or that victims of sexual assault "provoked" the attack by wearing attractive clothes, or by accompanying their acquaintance to a secluded place, or by hitchhiking. Some even go so far as to say that women actually want to be raped and seek the appropriate situation to satisfy such deep-seated craving. Others, who profess a more radical creed, do not hesitate to point out that, for examples, stores and not customers are responsible for shoplifting, because they display their wares in an enticing way.

In general, one can say that the distribution between the criminal and his victim—which in former days was deemed to be clear-cut—has become vague and blurred in individual cases. In particular, the relationship between the perpetrator and the victim has been determined to be much more intricate than the rough distinctions of "innocent versus guilty" acknowledged by criminal law. For example, it has been pointed out that even in cases of sex offenses when a minor is seduced by an adult "offender," the dynamics of the situation may be more complex than what society and the parents of the "victim" want to believe. In other words, adolescent sexuality is stronger than adults like to recognize, and the word "seduction" does not always accurately reflect what actually transpired in real life.

This approach to the explanation of crime and victimization is particularly attractive if one—accepting the officially reported rates of crimes—believes that most crime is localized in certain areas of the cities and affects a certain segment of the population. Then, one can easily see both criminals and victims as being of the same stock, predisposed to unlawfulness, provocative, and easily provoked. The same individuals may alternatively or even simultaneously be offenders and victims, while the majority of the population is safely outside, looking on with dismay, amusement, or indifference.

3. This refocusing of the dynamics of the crime situation has influenced policy making. In the past, the major emphasis in the war against crime was on punishment and deterrence. The goal was to affect the motivation of the offender by making it costly to engage in deviant behavior. Victim-centered research has changed this by pointing out the role of the victim in the commission of crimes. Other alternatives are now being proposed. Once the stereotype of the innocent and unsuspecting victim has been shelved, it has appeared reasonable to focus on the victim's behavior and to change it in order to effectively prevent crimes. Thus, pressure and incentives have been offered to potential victims to improve the safety and security of their dwellings, to adopt certain precautionary measures when leaving their homes for more than an hour, to use more sophisticated locks, to install television cameras in shops and banks, to hire private guards, to buy insurance, to engrave their most costly belongings with identification numbers, etc.

Thus, in some way, society has openly acknowledged that the victim plays a role in his own victimization and that by taking certain steps, he can avoid being victimized. It follows that if he is actually victimized, it may at least partially be his fault too. In other words, society has transferred part of the social cost and part of the blame from the criminal to the victim. In some countries, like Scandinavia, some have demanded a total transfer of such costs to the victim, when it was proposed, for example, that owners of supermarkets and department stores should not have the right to prosecute shoplifters and that banks should accept responsibility and absorb the loss for forged or bad checks. Thus, what is generally deemed to be crime, would be redefined as an occupational risk of which the banker or department store owner should be aware, and whose consequences they should be ready to accept without retaliation.

4. An important new perspective opened by victimological interest affects the operations of the criminal justice system. After what S. Schafer (1968) describes as "the golden age of the victim," the victim's input in the criminal justice system has been next to nil. Many feel that as a matter of fact, the victim is the most disregarded component in criminal justice proceedings.
After the victim has reported his victimization and has provided information to the police, he may not hear from the police or the prosecutor for long periods, or even not at all. There are cases where the case was disposed of without any consultation or contacting of the victim. If and when the victim is called for the trial, he falls into the category of witnesses—in this case, witnesses for the state—and is entitled to all the delays, postponements, and other frustrating experiences awaiting such persons at the courthouse.

The newly focused attention on the victim has brought to light the victim's plight at the hands of the criminal justice system. As a consequence, innovative proposals have been advanced calling, for example, for the creation of a victim's ombudsman; for the provision of legal and social referral services to the victim; for the right of the victim to be consulted and offer his inputs when the prosecutor engages in plea bargaining with the accused; and for a total revamping of the compensation-restitution idea. In the case of rape, the rapid and vocal development of the women's liberation movement has spurred victimologists—mostly males—to give more equitable and balanced attention to the issues surrounding what has been called "the most despicable but least punished" crime. Attention on the victim also calls for a reexamination of the whole issue of what is justice, what is crime, what is the appropriate remedy to victimization. Most—if not all—of the laws reflect a middle-class sense of values. Thus, justice, crime, punishment, and remedies rest on such middle-class foundations. But, most of the victims belong to the lower class. Consequently, there is an inherent inequity in the criminal justice system, since the opinions of one socioeconomic class dominate and dictate the perception, assessment, and disposition of matters deeply affecting another. Victimological research, therefore, is showing how the input of the victim should be sought when developing systems for the compensation of victims of crime, and how the concept of "relative loss" should be introduced in debate and deliberations for compensation (Anttila 1974).

Limitations and Risks of Research Focusing on the Victim

Research focusing on the victim will develop further and achieve further refinements and engineer new breakthroughs. However, there are some dangers that may develop as a consequence of victimological research.

1. It is possible that some researchers will simply shift their focus of attention from the individual criminal to the individual victim. This type of research would generate findings of little usefulness for decision makers, in that it would not take into account problems stemming from societal conditions and the cultural influences at large.

2. The growth of research focusing on the victim may involve a certain amount of distortion in what is actually selected as the object of inquiry. In other words, there may be an excessive concentration of interest and research efforts on crimes of violence, sexual offenses, and crimes of swindle. Some large groups of crimes have been neglected, one would suspect, mostly because there is no clearly identifiable victim. One could mention, for example, consumer-related issues; victims of omission and neglect rather than of commission; victims that are not identifiable individuals but organizations. In other words, it appears

as if victimologists have accepted the most common, less controversial, more easily applicable definition of who the victims are and who may be a victim. The current debate about consumer problems, the environment, poverty, and malnutrition, the inequitable distribution of wealth, the struggle of minorities and women to gain recognition and economic power, the failures of the justice system, the scandals surrounding the treatment of old people, the mentally retarded, the mentally ill, require that an enlarged list of victims receive the attention of criminologists and other scholars.

3. Although related to the preceding point, it is important to begin examining and studying victimization at the hand of the state and of the power structure. Again, most of the current victimological research falls along tradition-al lines of inquiry, focusing on individual-to-individual relationships rather than looking at the more diffuse and subtle—but by no means less important—rela-tionships of power and oppression. There is an urgent need to devote more attention to the recurrent instances of genocide, displacement, and persecution of select groups at the hand of other, more powerful ones; the various forms of colonialism; the misuse of psychiatric labels and facilities to suppress dissent and stifle opposition or unorthodox, innovative behavior; the acceptance and support of belief systems to justify oppression and discrimination. In other words, it is important for victimologists not to repeat the same errors of atomized thinking, researching, and theorizing that have characterized quite a portion of criminological research. Victimology has a bright future, if only corrective action is taken promptly to steer its development in the right direction.

References

Anttila, I. 1974. "Victimology: A New Territory in Criminology." *Scandinavian Studies in Criminology*, vol. 5 (1974).

Drapkin, I., and E. Viano. 1974. *Victimology*. Lexington, Mass.: Lexington Books, D.C. Heath and Co.

_____. 1974. *Victimology: A New Focus*. 5 volumes. Lexington, Mass.: Lexington Books, D.C. Heath and Co.

Ellenberger, H. 1954. "Relations Psychologiques Entre La Criminel et La Victime." *Revue Internationale de Criminologie et de Police Technique* 8, 1 (January-March): 103-121.

Fry, Margery. 1951. *Arms of the Law*. London: Gollancz.

Mendelsohn, Beniamin. 1956. "New Bio-psychosocial Horizons: Victimology." ("Nouvelle Branche de La Science Bio-psycho-sociale: La Victimologie.") *Revue Internationale de Criminologie et de Police Technique* 2: 107.

Schafer, S. 1968. *The Victim and His Criminal.* New York: Random House.

Von Hentig, Hans. 1940. "Remarks on the Interaction of Perpetrator and Victim." *Journal of Criminal Law and Criminology* 31 (September-October): 303-309.

_____. 1948. *The Criminal and His Victim.* New Haven, Conn.: Yale University Press.

The Elderly Victim: Vulnerability to the Criminal Act

John P.J. Dussich and
Charles J. Eichman

The battered child syndrome has been well researched and publicized but how much is known about the elderly victim syndrome?[a] Much of our lack of awareness regarding criminal victimization of the aged is due to a general paucity of victim data on all age groups (Midwest Research Institute 1975, p. 3). Although the systematic collection of victim data is not yet a reality, some major victimization surveys have recently been completed.

A major contributor to our lack of awareness of the elderly victim syndrome is the apparent reluctance of the mass media to portray senior citizens as being criminally victimized in proportion to the extent reported to the police. When a content analysis of one week's prime time network TV programming was conducted in New York in 1972, it was discovered that there had been no television murder victims over the age of 50, whereas the FBI Uniform Crime Reports, 1970, indicated that one-fifth of the murder victims in 1970 were in that age category (Dominick 1973).

Not all crime of the elderly is violent and spontaneous.

Some crime is subtle and calculated: the dance studio that preys on lonely widows, the ancient con game perpetrated by flim flam artists, the sale of land under water and useless hearing aids, and so forth. . . . They are pursued by heartless fortune hunters anxious to separate widows from their pittances. Those with visual handicaps are cheated when change is made in stores. Salesmen exploit them at the time of grief. Cosmetic firms make them feel ugly and extract their money in exchange for bringing "youth" to their faces. Quack doctors, appliances and drugs give them false hope. "Ethical" drug houses "tranquilize" them thus making illegitimate their natural anxieties and depressed moments—needed, in fact, to galvanize personal and collective action. Many of these more stark forms of prejudice and victimization are rarely subject to legal punishment. All of them occur in a general cultural framework that denies older people opportunities of obtaining work, decent housing, quality health care and a respectful place. (Brostoff et al. 1972, pp. 320-21, Reprinted with permission.)

In the sixties, the U.S. Senate Special Committee on Aging conducted a series of important hearings that publicized the vulnerability of older citizens to

Special thanks are extended to Carol Lunn who spent considerable time searching for data.

[a]The term *elderly victim syndrome* is proposed for the group of victimizations and predispositions to which the elderly seem especially vulnerable. "Syndrome" is employed in its meaning of "concurrence," referring to the constellation of antecedent and consequential factors characterizing the aged victim.

medical quackery, misleading health insurance schemes, and other deceptions and frauds. The published hearings and committee reports contain extensive information on the dimensions of unethical and illegal practices that were bilking millions of dollars annually from the nation's senior citizens (Senate Special Committee 1963; 1964; 1965; 1967).

A recurring and as yet unresolved question is whether the elderly are disproportionately victimized in comparison with other age groups. A typical assertion in this vein is that "the aged as a group are especially vulnerable to being criminally victimized" (Gubrium 1972, p. 293).

In an attempt to further understand the victimization of the elderly, a number of victimization studies have been conducted in some of our larger cities. In a Washington, D.C. study sponsored by the Washington School of Psychiatry in 1970, police furnished the names of elderly crime victims to project social workers. Robbery was the most frequent crime. In addition, old people were often the victims of purse snatching and mail-box thefts of their social security, public assistance, and pension checks (Brostoff et al. 1972, p. 320).

A recently completed survey in Houston has indicated that for most crimes, the aged are not overvictimized when compared with persons under 65 years of age. However, the elderly do have a higher victimization rate for robbery, swindling, and purse snatching (Forston and Kitchens 1974, p. 32). In contrast, Phyllis Mensh Brostoff et al. reported in a 1970 Washington, D.C. study that the elderly are disproportionately victimized by criminals—25 percent of the population of the nation's capitol, but 32 percent of its crime victims, were over 50 (1972, p. 319).

In an elderly victim study currently underway in Kansas City, an interim report shows the crime that poses the greatest threat to the elderly is burglary. Of 1,831 crimes against the elderly, 55.9 percent were burglary (Midwest Research Institute, 1975, pp. 3-4).

Other studies have also shed light on the extent to which the aged are victimized. The 1972 Denver Victimization Survey concluded, "The relationship between rates of personal victimizations and the victim's age can be described as an increase from the lowest age group (12-15) to the next group (16-19) and then a decrease through the entire age range." A declining slope holds for each of the major crime categories beginning at age 20—rape, robbery, assault, and personal larceny (Carr et al., 1974, p. 68).

In the nation's five largest cities, the victimization rate for the elderly (age 50 and over) was highest for personal larceny without physical contact and lowest for rape. Compared with the other age groups, in most cities the elderly had the lowest victimization rates for the crimes of rape, robbery, assault, and personal larceny[b] (LEAA 1974b, pp. 11-15).

[b]*Personal larceny* is equivalent to personal crimes of theft. *Personal larceny with contact* is the theft of purse, wallet, or cash by stealth directly from the person of the victim, but without force or the threat of force. It also includes attempted purse snatching. *Personal larceny without contact* is the theft, without direct contact between victim and offender, of property or cash from any place other than the victim's home or its immediate vicinity. It also includes attempted theft.

In a 1974 report on a national victimization survey being conducted by the National Crime Panel, it was affirmed that those 65 and over have the lowest victimization rate of any age category. Of the six crimes studied for those 65 and over, both sexes were victimized the most by personal larceny (LEAA 1974a, pp. 18-21).

A possible explanation for the general view that the elderly are disproportionately victimized is, as George Sunderland points out, that the elderly have an inordinate fear of murder and rape, although statistics indicate they have a very low chance of becoming victims of these crimes (1975, p. 91). From the various victimization surveys currently available, it appears that although most studies suggest the same pattern of undervictimization, some variations in the kinds of victimization are evident with different geographic locations.

Definition

In general studies of the elderly, one realizes that this group is unique in a variety of ways; one of these ways is their unique vulnerability to certain crimes. *Vulnerability* refers to the state or property of being open to attack or damage (Webster 1969, p. 999). Vulnerability suggests at least three types of targets: *personal*, which would include the possibility of physical and emotional injury; *financial*, which would include the potential loss of income, savings, and earning capacity, and; *material*, which would include the likelihood of damage to real property.

Vulnerability may be said to exist in two modes or conditions, passive and active. *Passive vulnerability* refers to a condition whereby a victim's status, for example, age, sex, income, race, stature, etc. is recognized as exploitable. *Active vulnerability* refers to a condition whereby a victim's behavior, for example, demure, seductive, aggressive, antagonistic, etc., contributes interactionally to a crime (Dussich 1975). This is similar to Marvin Wolfgang's notion of "victim precipitated" crimes (1970, pp. 569-78). An example of passive vulnerability is depicted by John Lofland in explaining the interaction between offenders and victims, where the offenders claim their victims deserve to be injured due to their "consensually viewed" lower status (Communists, homosexuals, the elderly, drunks, etc.) (1969, p. 90).

Lofland typified active vulnerability in discussing yet another category of "deserved" victims, which may result from a history of a very personal nature between persons who interact as *individuals* rather than as members of socially stigmatized categories—especially in homicides.

Theory

In 1971, J.F. Gubrium proposed what was termed a new socioenvironmental theory of aging. Essentially, he suggested two factors: the degree of age homogeneity in one's social environment and the person's capacity (resources) to engage in varied and flexible activities. He predicted that elderly persons will have high morale (1) when *high* individual resources for flexible activities coincide with a social environment that is age heterogeneous, and (2) when *low* individual resources for flexible activities coincide with a social environment that is age homogeneous (Gubrium 1972, pp. 281-84).

In the final paragraphs of his article, Gubrium turned his attention to the question of how elderly crime victims are selected. He began with the assumption that "the likelihood of being victimized varies directly with personal visibility." Then he predicted that the two sets of conditions creating higher levels of morale among the aged will also create lower visibility and thus result in lower vulnerability to criminal victimization.

In the opinion of the authors, Gubrium's visibility paradigm seems plausible. Certainly in an age-heterogeneous environment, the aged person who is healthier and wealthier and more mobile will blend in better. Similarly, in an age-homogeneous environment, the aged person who is of poor health and impecunious means will fit in relatively well. That the opposite combinations will produce subjects of high relative visibility seems equally plausible.

However, in the authors' opinion, Gubrium seems most open to criticism on his initial assumption that the probability of being victimized varies directly with personal visibility. At best, visibility is only one of myriad factors influencing the offender's choice of a victim. There is reason to suspect that such criteria may vary widely with the potential offense. In many crimes, a highly visible victim would be a distinct liability. Without some convincing rationale or empirical basis for believing that visibility is indeed linked directly with vulnerability, Gubrium's hypothesis regarding victim selection among the aged seems to us to be questionable.

In the search for a plausible explanation of vulnerability it was realized that, besides Gubrium, very little has been done. Thus, one of the authors (Dussich 1975) offers the following statements concerning vulnerability which are relevant to the victimization of the elderly:

1. In order for vulnerability to be a consideration in victimization, it must be obtrusive in nature, that is, the vulnerability (passive or active) must be obvious to the prospective offender.
2. Vulnerability of the aged is, for the most part, unobtrusive in nature, that is, the life-styles of most elderly persons reduce the degree to which their actual vulnerability is blatant.
3. Unobtrusive vulnerability inhibits victimization of the elderly, especially with regard to personal crimes.

In support of the above statements it must first be mentioned that lack of reporting among the aged is *not* a valid argument for disclaiming the validity of crime statistics of the elderly. It has been found that the elderly report personal crimes in slightly greater proportion than other age groups (LEAA 1975, p. 29).

With regard to personal crimes against the elderly, studies indicate that the elderly are undervictimized for the personal crimes of murder, rape, and assault, but not for robbery when the elderly live in high crime areas. With regard to property crimes against the elderly, studies indicate diminishing victimization with age, excluding burglary and purse snatching in high crime areas (Forston and Kitchens 1974; Brostoff et al. 1972; Midwest Research Institute 1975; Carr et al. 1974; LEAA 1974a; 1974c).

The unobtrusive vulnerability of the aged with regard to personal crime effectively protects them, as their mobility is restricted, and they are often isolated from public interaction. The only instances when their vulnerability is obtrusive is when they must leave their isolation, and personal encounters take place. This condition results in the overvictimization of the elderly for the crimes of robbery and purse snatching. Robbery and purse snatching require the aged to leave their dwelling; swindling usually takes place in a victim's home (Forston and Kitchens 1974, p. 29). This condition results when the prospective offender is invited into the home and the elderly person's vulnerabilities are open to close scrutiny.

Special Studies

Alarmed that 25 percent of the population of Washington, D.C., but 32 percent of its crime victims, were over 50, the Washington School of Psychiatry sponsored a 1970 demonstration study to respond to affected elderly persons. Project Assist, an eight-month undertaking, studied the extent of victimization among the aged and formulated a model for establishing a program of police-community relations designed to benefit the elderly (Brostoff et al. 1972).[c] A social worker with training in community organization helped to coordinate police contacts with community organizations and resources. The police in one district of Washington, D.C. supplied the project staff with the names of elderly persons who had reported crimes they had suffered or who were experiencing other social crises.

Project Assist served 220 clients whose mean age was 70. Sixty-three percent were female. Black victims outnumbered white victims, although in the District of Columbia there were more whites than blacks after the sixth decade of life. About one-fifth had multiple social problems. "Many of the sample were physically and/or mentally impaired in some serious way, adding to their vulnerability to crime and social problems." Widowed, single persons, and the poor on assistance were disproportionately represented. One-third had no telephone. Concluded the Project Assist staff, "Clearly, to be old and poor and

[c]See Chapter 14 for a full discussion of Project Assist.

widowed and a woman increases the chances for police contact" by some considerable degree (Brostoff et al. 1972, p. 320).

In the crime-ridden Strawberry Mansion section of Philadelphia elderly immigrant Jews must cope with an unrelenting and hostile environment:

The husband of one of our researchers . . . quickly learned the adaptive tricks required of the ghetto dweller: "I avoided streetcorners where youngsters were lurking. I avoided noisy groups outside bars. At night, I kept to the busiest and best-lighted streets, and walked near the curb."

For older people it is not so easy. They live near these bars, the streetcorners lie between their home and the grocery, and at night it would be unthinkable to go out. The aridness of the area is intensified by the fact that there is no bank, no post office, no supermarket, and no hospital in the area (Lawton and Kleban 1971, p. 278, Reprinted with permission.)

Thus, not only has biological aging brought about individual changes that make the elderly seem like easy prey, but ecological succession within the residents' community has brought about changes in the demographics and the environment that further endanger the elderly. The Strawberry Mansion aged had fewer friends and fewer neighbors. A very large percentage (78%) reported being dissatisfied with their level of social interaction, compared with a rate of 34 percent in comparable housing groups.

In summary, the elderly residents of the Strawberry Mansion section, compared with national data, were more often single and widowed, were more often foreign-born, and had a much lower income. M. Powell Lawton and Morton Kleban found they were deprived in the areas of health, neighborhood mobility, leisure-time activity, peer interaction, morale, and housing satisfaction. On top of these handicaps and vulnerabilities is the aggravating condition of the area's overwhelming crime problem. Lawton and Kleban asked why an elderly person would choose to remain in such an extremely noxious environment:

At least one major reason why he does not move is that his very low rent, or home ownership, together with his low income, lock him in. His life space is grossly restricted, ordinary coping behavior requires energy expenditure at a near-upper threshold level, and he cannot escape (Lawton and Kleban 1971, p. 280, Reprinted with permission.)

It is clear that much more research needs to be conducted in the area of differential vulnerability of the aged. If strategies are to be developed to protect our elderly citizens from criminal victimization, they must be based on fact and not on fiction.

References

Brostoff, Phyllis Mensh, Roberta B. Brown, and Robert N. Butler. 1972. "The Public Interest: Report No. 6. 'Beating Up' on the Elderly: Police, Social Work, Crime." *International Journal of Aging and Human Development*, 3, 4319-22. © Baywood Publishing Company.

Carr, John D., T.A. Giacinti, P.M. McCullough, and M.J. Molof. 1974. *Analysis of 1972 Denver Victimization Survey.* (High Impact Anti-Crime Program). Denver: Denver Anti-Crime Council, 1974.

Dominick, Joseph R. 1973. "Crime and Law Enforcement on Prime-Time Television." Public Opinion Quarterly, 37, 241-50.

Dussich, John P.J. 1975. Unpublished notes.

Forston, Raymon, and James Kitchens. 1974. *Criminal Victimization of the Aged: The Houston Model Neighborhood Area.* Denton, Texas: Center for Community Services, North Texas State University.

Gubrium, Jaber F. 1972. "Toward a Socio-Environmental Theory of Aging." *The Gerontologist*, 12, 281-84.

Lawton, M. Powell, and Morton H. Kleban. 1971. "The Aged Resident of the Inner City." *The Gerontologist*, 11, 277-83.

LEAA (U.S. Department of Justice, Law Enforcement Assistance Administration). 1973. *Sourcebook of Criminal Justice Statistics: 1973.* Washington, D.C.: U.S. Government Printing Office.

_____. 1974a. *Crimes and Victims: A Report on the Dayton-San Jose Pilot Survey of Victimization.* Washington, D.C.: U.S. Government Printing Office.

_____. 1974b. *Crime in the Nation's Five Largest Cities.* (Advance Report.) Washington, D.C.: U.S. Government Printing Office.

_____. 1974c. *Criminal Victimization in the United States.* January-June, 1973. Washington, D.C.: U.S. Government Printing Office.

_____. 1975. *Criminal Victimization Surveys in the Nation's Five Largest Cities.* Washington, D.C.: U.S. Government Printing Office.

Lofland, John. 1969. *Deviance and Identity.* Englewood Cliffs, N.J.: Prentice-Hall.

Midwest Research Institute. 1975. *Crimes against Aging Americans: The Kansas City Study.* Kansas City: Midwest Research Institute.

Senate Special Committee on Aging (U.S.). 1963. *Frauds and Quackery Affecting the Older Citizen.* Washington, D.C.: U.S. Government Printing Office.

_____. 1964. *Deceptive or Misleading Methods in Health Insurance Sales.* Washington, D.C.: U.S. Government Printing Office.

_____. 1965. *Frauds and Deceptions Affecting the Elderly: Investigations, Findings, and Recommendations: 1964.* Washington, D.C.: U.S. Government Printing Office.

_____. 1967. *Consumer Interests of the Elderly.* Washington, D.C.: U.S. Government Printing Office.

Sunderland, George. 1975. "Crime Prevention for the Elderly." *Ekistics*, 39 (231), 91-92.

Webster's Seventh New Collegiate Dictionary. 1969. Springfield, Mass.: Merriam-Webster.

Wolfgang, Marvin E. 1970. "Victim-precipitated Criminal Homicide." In: M.E. Wolfgang, L. Savitz, and N. Johnston, *The Sociology of Crime and Delinquency* (2nd Edition). New York: Wiley and Sons, 569-78.

10 Robbery, the Elderly, and Fear: An Urban Problem in Search of Solution

John E. Conklin

Robbery is the use or threat of force against an individual in order to steal from him. Because it involves both the danger of physical harm and the loss of property, it is doubly alarming. Additionally, a higher proportion of robberies than of other violent crimes is committed by strangers to the victims; Lynn Curtis (1974, pp. 46-47) found that about four of every five robberies in 17 large American cities in 1967 were perpetrated by strangers. Hence, robbery is a "bellwether" crime, an indicator of both contemporary crime and contemporary fears.

The elderly in the United States, particularly those who live in large cities and in housing projects, are highly vulnerable to robbery. Robbers, especially young and inexperienced ones, seek victims who are older, physically weak, or alone (Conklin 1972, pp. 89-91). The elderly are thus vulnerable for several reasons: they are physically weaker than younger people, include a disproportionately large number of women, and are more likely to live alone because of the higher probability that a spouse will have died and that no children will be living with them.

In this chapter, we first examine the crime of robbery among the elderly. Next, the elderly's reaction to crime and the consequences of those reactions are explored. In conclusion, some suggestions for minimizing the risk of robbery among the elderly and for breaking into a self-reinforcing cycle of crime and fear are presented.

Robbery among the Elderly

In 1969-70, the author, under the auspices of the Center for Criminal Justice at Harvard Law School, conducted a study of robbery in Boston in 1964 and 1968. Only the 1968 data are examined here. All police reports from the first six months of that year were coded for information about the robbery incident, the offender, and the victim. The Boston Police Department recorded 847 cases of robbery during this period. The age of the victim was mentioned in 754, or 89 percent, of those cases. Only this group of 754 cases are analyzed in this chapter. For purposes of looking at "the elderly," we have compared those under 60 years old (587 cases, or 77.9 percent of the 754 cases) with those 60 years old

The data in this chapter were gathered in a research project at the Center for Criminal Justice at Harvard Law School during 1969-70.

and over (167 cases, and 22.1 percent of the 754 cases). Such a definition provides us with enough robberies of older people to compare with robberies of younger victims.

Before comparing elderly victims and younger victims, we consider the crude rates of victimization for different age groups. The preference of robbers for vulnerable victims (Conklin 1972, pp. 87-97) and the great fear of the elderly for their safety (see below) suggest a high rate of victimization among the elderly. However, this fear might lead the elderly to take defensive measures, for example, to stay indoors, to walk outside only in groups, or to move to safer neighborhoods. If such special measures are taken by the elderly, their victimization rate might be reduced below what it would be if their behavior patterns were similar to the rest of the population.

Column D of Table 10-1 indicates the elderly do not have excessively high rates of robbery, when all types of robbery are considered. However, since a large proportion of those over 60 are retired, unemployed, or disabled, one must consider separately robberies of individuals in noncommercial roles in order to obtain a more accurate indicator of the risk individuals face in daily life. Column F clearly shows that rates of robbery victimization in street holdups, purse

Table 10-1
Rates of Victimization in Robberies

(A)	(B)	(C)	(D)	(E)	(F)
Age Groups	Number in Boston Population, 1970	Number of Robberies, 1968	1968 Rate of Robbery	Number of Individual[a] Robberies, 1968	1968 Rate of Individual Robberies
0-9	101,634	0	0.0	0	0.0
10-19	112,122	88	78.5	63	56.2
20-29	125,043	177	141.6	99	79.2
30-39	60,562	93	153.6	48	79.3
40-49	64,433	106	164.5	64	99.3
50-59	64,763	122	188.4	52	80.3
60-69	57,646	94	163.1	58	100.6
70 and over	54,868	72	131.2	60	109.4
Total	641,071	752	117.3	444	69.3

Note: The numbers of robberies and the rates of victimization are calculated using robberies from the first six months of 1968, so the rates are per 100,000 people for a six-month period. The rates for the last six months of 1968 would be considerably higher, since the period including 1968 was a time of rapidly escalating robbery rates in Boston. There were 847 robberies in the first six months of 1968, but 1,313 recorded cases in the last half of the year.

[a]Individual robberies include street robberies, purse snatches recorded as robberies by the police, and robberies in the home.

snatches, and residential robberies do rise with increasing age. Citizens who are 70 years old and over have a victimization rate in these crimes that is more than 50 percent higher than the rate for the total population. These figures confirm that the elderly have a higher robbery rate, although one that may be reduced by the effectiveness of certain self-protective measures.

Not only do those 60 years old and over have a higher rate of noncommercial robbery, but the nature of the robberies in which elderly victims are involved differs from the nature of robberies of younger victims. Table 10-2 shows some of those differences.

Elderly victims are more often held up by young[a] robbers than are victims under the age of 60. Sections A and B of Table 10-2 show that robberies of the elderly more often involve offenders in the 10-19-year-old group and more often involve offenders who are legally juveniles. Elderly victims are also more often held up by blacks than are younger victims.[b] The elderly victims are also slightly more likely than younger victims to be robbed by multiple offenders, although this relationship was not statistically significant. These variables are linked. As described elsewhere (Conklin 1972, pp. 63-71), the opportunist pattern of robbery involves unplanned attacks on accessible and vulnerable citizens; this pattern is typical of loosely knit groups of younger blacks. In contrast stands the professional pattern of carefully planned robberies of commercial establishments, which is more common among well-organized groups of somewhat older whites.

Most robbery victims are alone when attacked. However, section E of Table 10-2 shows that the elderly are even more apt to be alone than are younger victims. This is not entirely expected, since the relative weakness of the elderly might make even groups of older people vulnerable, whereas the stronger and younger victims might be robbed only if they were alone. Possibly, the dual vulnerability of the aged that results from their being both weak and alone strikes some "marginal" and uncommitted offenders as an opportunity that is "too good to pass up."

Elderly victims are more apt than younger ones to be victims of noncom-

---

[a]Ages of offenders were calculated by using the victim's estimate of the offender's age that appeared in most police reports. With multiple offenders, the average estimated age was used. The use of such estimates provides a larger group for analysis than would the use of cases with arrested suspects.

[b]The 1968 Boston robbery reports provided evidence of race of both offender and victim in only 31.6 percent of the 847 cases. Of those 268 robberies, 65.3 percent involved black offender and white victim, 1.9 percent white offender and black victim, 17.7 percent black offender and black victim, and 15.3 percent white offender and white victim. The 1967 national study by Curtis (1974, p. 21) found corresponding percentages of 46.7, 1.7, 38.4, and 13.2 for armed robberies, and 43.9, 1.1, 37.1, and 17.9 for unarmed robberies. However, these percentages are based on only 52.8 percent of the armed robbery cases and 50.0 percent of the unarmed robbery cases. In both the national study and the Boston study, the absence of police data on race in many cases raises the possibility of selective bias in the recording of those data.

Table 10-2
Characteristics of Robberies Involving the Elderly and Other Victims

Characteristic of Robbery	Under 60	60 and Over	Level of Significance
A. Estimated age of offender			
10-19	31.0%	42.3%	
20-29	53.5%	48.0%	
30 and over	15.5%	9.8%	$\psi^2 = 6.37$
Total number	419	123	$p < 0.05$
B. Estimated age status of offender			
Juvenile (under 17)	11.2%	23.6%	
Adult (17 and over)	88.8%	76.4%	$\psi^2 = 12.18$
Total number	419	123	$p < 0.001$
C. Race of offender			
White	35.6%	16.3%	
Black	64.4%	83.8%	$\psi^2 = 35.92$
Total number	533	160	$p < 0.001$
D. Number of offenders			
One	37.9%	34.3%	
Two or more	62.1%	65.6%	$\psi^2 = 0.83$
Total number	585	166	Not significant
E. Number of victims			
One	89.3%	94.6%	
Two or more	10.7%	5.4%	$\psi^2 = 4.35$
Total number	587	167	$p < 0.05$
F. Type of robbery			
Street	42.0%	30.5%	
Purse snatch	9.8%	25.0%	
Home	7.2%	16.5%	
Taxicab	17.9%	12.2%	
Commercial	23.1%	15.9%	$\psi^2 = 43.56$
Total number	553	164	$p < 0.001$
G. Victim resistance[a]			
Some	18.6%	11.0%	
None	81.4%	89.0%	$\psi^2 = 2.07$
Total number	236	73	Not significant
H. Victim resistance[b]			
Some	7.6%	4.9%	
None	92.4%	95.1%	$\psi^2 = 1.12$
Total number	582	164	Not significant
I. Force used by offender			
No force used	41.6%	26.9%	
Told victim to lie down or			
removed victim from scene	8.4%	2.5%	

Table 10-2 (cont.)

Characteristic of Robbery	Under 60	60 and Over	Level of Significance
Shoved, pushed, or knocked to ground	27.6%	48.8%	
Beat, punched, or hit with a weapon	17.3%	15.0%	
Cut, stabbed, or shot with a weapon	5.1%	6.9%	$\psi^2 = 30.80$
Total number	514	160	$p < 0.001$
J. Injury to victim			
None	74.8%	58.2%	
Some, without hospital treatment	5.5%	14.4%	
Some, with hospital treatmen	19.7%	27.5%	$\psi^2 = 18.81$
Total number	523	153	$p < 0.001$

[a]Resistance was coded "None" only if the police report specifically mentioned the absence of victim resistance.

[b]Resistance was coded "None" if no mention of actual victim resistance appeared in the police report.

mercial holdups because fewer of them are working. Looking at all commercial robberies (including taxicab holdups), we find from section F of Table 10-2 that 28.1 percent of the elderly victims and 41.0 percent of the younger victims were involved in commercial robberies. Street robberies, exclusive of handbag snatches, were more common among younger victims. However, purse snatches were much more common among elderly victims.[c] This cannot be accounted for solely by the different sex ratios in the younger and older age groups. If street robberies and purse snatches are added together, a slightly larger proportion of the elderly victims are involved in such holdups than is true of younger victims. Elderly victims were more often than younger victims involved in residential robberies. In selecting a target for a burglary, offenders who are aware of the occupancy of a building by an elderly person may not be deterred, figuring that such a person will provide no resistance to theft. This might result in a residential robbery. On the other hand, burglars might be more concerned about the occupancy of a dwelling by a younger person, preferring to avoid the confrontation and a robbery.

Being older, weaker, alone, and facing younger and stronger offenders, one might expect the elderly victim to resist on rare occasion. Looking at only those

[c]The police can classify a purse snatch as a robbery or a larceny, depending on whether force is used. Since this is often difficult to determine, one might expect the greater weakness of the elderly would lead the police to record a higher proportion of purse snatches with elderly victims as robberies, in contrast to those involving younger victims. This is not the case. Of the 71 purse snatches (both robberies and larcenies) in the first six months of 1968 that involved victims under the age of 60, 38.0 percent were recorded as robberies; of the 63 purse snatches that involved victims 60 years old and over, 38.1 percent were recorded as robberies.

police reports where the presence or absence of victim resistance is specifically mentioned, we found that about one of nine elderly victims did resist in some way, a smaller proportion than for younger victims. This relationship was not statistically significant. If one assumes that when a police report fails to mention any victim resistance, none has occurred, only about 1 elderly victim in 20 resists, compared with about 1 in 14 of the younger victims.

In spite of the absence of resistance from elderly victims, their assailants were more apt to use force than were the robbers of younger victims. However, such force usually involved shoving, pushing, or knocking down the victim rather than beating, knifing, or shooting him. Nevertheless, 21.9 percent of the elderly victims and 22.4 percent of the younger victims did suffer such violence.

As expected from the more frequent physical contact between offender and victim, elderly victims were more often and more severely injured. Whereas 25.2 percent of the younger victims were injured and 19.7 percent of them received hospital treatment, the corresponding figures for elderly victims were 41.9 percent and 27.5 percent. Although they resisted less often, elderly victims more frequently met violence and more often suffered injuries severe enough to require hospital treatment.

The pattern of robbery of the elderly is more threatening than the pattern of robbery of younger victims. The offender is more often young, black, and works with accomplices. The victim is more often alone. Although the elderly victim resists less often than younger ones, force is more often used by the offender and physical injury more often sustained by the victim. If crime, and robbery in particular, is feared more by the elderly than by the young, this is not only because the elderly feel more vulnerable because they are weak or alone. Evidence indicates that the robberies they suffer are objectively more threatening than the robberies suffered by younger victims.

Fear of Crime among the Elderly

Although robbery is representative of contemporary crime and contemporary fears because it combines the loss of property with a direct and possibly violent confrontation with a stranger, it is only part of the crime problem faced by the elderly. They also confront burglary, larceny, auto theft, and other "traditional" offenses, as well as consumer fraud and other white-collar crimes. In this section, we explore the reactions to crime of the elderly in two Boston-area communities. One community is a suburb with a low crime rate; the other is an urban community with a relatively high crime rate. These communities and the samples of residents interviewed in each are described elsewhere (Conklin 1975, pp. 251-58). For purposes of analysis, we have divided each sample into three age groups, which we refer to as young (20 to 39 years old), middle (40 to 59 years old), and old (60 years old and over).

People of all ages in the high crime rate urban community perceived more crime in their community than did residents of the low crime rate suburb (see section A of Table 10-3). Within each community, there was no clear relationship between age and perception of crime; that is, residents of each community perceived similar amounts of crime in the area, regardless of their age. The elderly thus do not differ from younger residents in their assessment of how much crime there is in the community, although elderly residents of the high crime rate area do perceive more crime in their area than do the elderly residents of the low crime rate suburb.

Section B of Table 10-3 shows that residents of the high crime rate area feel less safe than those who live in the low crime rate area, regardless of age. Within each area, the elderly feel somewhat less safe than the younger residents. In other words, the elderly perceive no more crime in their community than do younger residents, but they do feel less safe. Apparently they feel more vulnerable; the accuracy of this perception is supported by the more objective evidence presented in the first section of this chapter.

For the total sample from the high crime rate area, there was an inverse relationship between perception of crime and perception of safety: those who perceived more crime in their area felt less safe there. However, no such relationship emerged in the low crime rate area; that is, perception of crime was unrelated to feelings of safety in the suburb. Evidently, crime and the perception of crime in that area had not passed the critical threshold necessary for perception of crime to affect feelings of safety. This suggests that those who live in high crime areas, including the elderly, will have their feelings of safety more influenced by how much crime they perceive than will those who live in objectively low crime rate areas but who feel there is a high crime rate there.

Residents of the high crime rate area also express less trust of others than do residents of the low crime rate area, whatever their age. There is no relationship of interpersonal trust to age in the low crime rate area, but those 60 years old and over living in the high crime rate area are somewhat less trusting of others than are the younger residents of that community.

Trust of others was inversely related to perception of crime (the more trust, the less crime perceived) and directly related to perceived safety (the more trust, the more perceived safety) in the high crime rate area. In the low crime rate suburb, there was no relationship between trust of others and either perceived amount of crime in the community or perceived safety. Again the threshold effect is seen; when crime and its perception pass a certain level, as in the high crime rate urban community, interpersonal trust is adversely affected.

Residents of the high crime rate community, whatever their age, express fewer positive feelings for their community than do the residents of the low crime rate community. Within each community, the elderly express more positive feelings for their community than do the younger residents of the community. This is somewhat surprising in light of the fact that they feel less

Table 10-3

Reactions to Crime in a High Crime Rate Community and a Low Crime Rate Community

Reaction to Crime	Low Crime Rate Community	High Crime Rate Community
A. Perception of crime[a]		
Young (20-39)	1.16 (42)	1.77 (35)
Middle (40-59)	1.17 (49)	1.50 (46)
Old (60 and over)	1.08 (33)	1.69 (24)
B. Perception of safety[b]		
Young (20-39)	2.48 (44)	2.06 (41)
Middle (40-59)	2.42 (56)	2.07 (56)
Old (60 and over)	2.24 (38)	1.86 (31)
C. Interpersonal trust[c]		
Young (20-39)	3.61 (44)	3.24 (40)
Middle (40-59)	3.51 (56)	3.19 (56)
Old (60 and over)	3.77 (36)	3.10 (31)
D. Affect for the community[d]		
Young (20-39)	2.38 (43)	1.96 (41)
Middle (40-59)	2.68 (56)	2.16 (56)
Old (60 and over)	2.77 (37)	2.32 (31)
E. Number of crimes respondents willing to report to police[e]		
Young (20-39)	9.77 (44)	9.05 (41)
Middle (40-59)	9.46 (56)	8.38 (56)
Old (60 and over)	8.92 (38)	7.61 (31)

[a]The range of this scale is from one to three, with one being less crime perceived and three being more crime perceived. Three questions were used in the construction of this scale.

[b]The range of this scale is from one to three, with one being less perceived safety and three being more perceived safety. Six questions were used in the construction of this scale.

[c]The range of this scale is from one to five, with one being the least amount of interpersonal trust and five being the most interpersonal trust. Four questions were used in the construction of this scale.

[d]The range of this scale is from one to three, with one being less positive affect for the community and three being more positive affect for the community. Four questions were used in the construction of this scale.

[e]The numbers are the total average number of crimes respondents said they were willing to report to the police, from among 13 crimes about which each respondent was questioned.

Source: John E. Conklin, *The Impact of Crime*. New York: Macmillan Publishing Co., Inc., 1975, pp. 260-266. Reprinted with permission.

safe in their community. Evidently, familiarity that comes from long-term residence in the community offsets the threat of crime when elderly respondents are asked about their general feelings toward their community.

In the high crime rate urban community, positive affect for the community is lowest among those who perceive most crime in the area, those who feel least safe in the area, and those who express least interpersonal trust. In the low crime rate suburb, no relationship of affect to these three measures emerges. Again, we see the threshold effect in operation.

Residents of the high crime rate community who perceive more crime in the area feel less safe, less trusting, and less positive toward their community than do residents of the community who perceive less crime. In the low crime rate community, perception of crime is not related to safety, trust, or affect for the community. The elderly in the high crime rate area feel less safe and less trusting than other residents, but they like their community more than do the younger residents.

Fear of crime has a number of important ramifications. For one, it leads to certain defensive measures (Furstenberg 1972; Conklin 1975, pp. 105-30). People seek to enhance their security with alarm systems, locks, bars, lights, firearms, and watchdogs. These "target-hardening" measures are often costly, especially for the elderly who often live on reduced incomes. Such measures may protect specific individuals while shifting crime to less well-protected targets. These measures also erect barriers between individuals and draw attention to the inability of the government and the police to protect citizens.

People who live in fear of crime will avoid certain areas of the city at night, use taxis or cars when they go out, maintain a distance from strangers, or stay home. This behavior, which is especially common in high crime rate areas (Furstenberg 1972), severely restricts mobility and creates great inconvenience. The elderly, who feel even less safe than other residents of high crime areas, may thus become "prisoners in their own homes" (Conklin 1975, p. 109). The Boston study found no differences in perception of local crime rates by age of the respondent, but did find a slight difference in perceived safety by age. In a survey of Baltimore residents, Frank Furstenberg (1972) found that older men or women were more apt to use "avoidance techniques" than were younger men or women, although they did not express more fear of crime. He suggests that the young may be less willing than older people to adjust their daily lives to the threat of crime. This may be because the elderly, who fear crime to the same extent as younger people, think they are less likely to survive an assault or a robbery without severe injury; the young may feel they can better take care of themselves in such situations. Evidence that the elderly do adjust their lives to the threat of crime comes from a newspaper report that a hearing of the Special Senate Committee on Aging was poorly attended by the invited elderly because few dared brave the streets to get to the hearing room (see Conklin 1975, pp. 109-10).

The isolation of the elderly reduces their access to services. One resident of a housing project claims, "Doctors won't make house calls, stores won't deliver goods, cabs won't make calls, movers are afraid to come in, sometimes the ambulance won't come and the undertaker is afraid to come to remove the deceased" (Conklin 1975, p. 110). The elderly, especially those in housing projects, are effectively cut off from outside goods and services. However, criminals may take advantage of this isolation to rob the elderly in their homes or burglarize their apartments. On occasion, offenders have even posed as maintenance men, deliverymen, or agents of service organizations in order to gain entrance to the homes of the elderly (Conklin 1975, p. 110). Victimization in this way will reinforce suspicions and fears and decrease openness to further contact with strangers.

People who live in high crime rate areas are fearful, suspicious, and distrustful. They avoid strangers and do not seek to make friends of unknown neighbors. This weakens social ties and diminishes the informal social control of crime in the community. In the absence of clear community norms about crime and community action to enforce those norms, offenders will feel safe to engage in crime in the area. On the other hand, social solidarity in the community which manifests itself in greater social interaction among residents in public places, will provide more surveillance of behavior in the area. If reinforced by a willingness to report crime to the police and to take direct personal action to prevent crime, such surveillance will constrain potential offenders, although they may shift to targets in less well-protected places. Fear of crime, by its effects on attitudes and social behavior, may thus contribute to the crime problem by reducing informal social control that would otherwise constrain offenders.

Fear of crime also leads the public to rely on the police to stop crime. This often takes the form of leaving all law enforcement to the police. In contrast to the residents of the low crime rate suburb, the residents of the high crime rate Boston community were less willing to call the police to report crime (see section E of Table 10-3) and more likely to feel that crime fighting was a job for the police and not the public. Within both communities, those who perceived higher crime rates in the area were apt to say they would report fewer crimes to the police than those who perceived lower local crime rates.

Although the elderly in these two communities did not perceive more or less crime than the younger residents, in each community they did express somewhat greater concern for their personal safety. Section E of Table 10-3 shows that the elderly were also willing to report fewer offenses to the police than were the younger residents. One reason may be a fear of reprisals from the offenders; perceived vulnerability may have reduced willingness to make a public issue of private suffering. Also, fear of crime may have led the elderly to excessive reliance on the police, seeing them as omnipotent rather than in need of public cooperation. In a national survey reported by Joe Feagin (1970), older people were less apt than younger ones to feel that private citizens had to be prepared to defend their homes from crime because of the inadequacy of the police. The elderly apparently react to their fear of crime by placing the responsibility for crime-fighting on the police and by withdrawing from social contact for self-protection. Their response is rarely an aggressive one, as can be seen from a survey by Marx and Archer (1972) in which the elderly were less apt to support and less willing to join civilian police patrols than were younger respondents.

Conclusions

The elderly have a higher rate of robbery victimization than younger people. In contrast to younger victims, the nature of robberies suffered by the elderly is more threatening—it more often involves younger offenders who rob in groups of two or more, solitary victims, the use of force, and physical injury. The fear generated by robbery and other crimes dramatically changes the life of the elderly. Barriers are erected between people by the avoidance of strangers and by security measures. Diminished social interaction reduces surveillance of public places. The resulting reduction in informal social control makes crime a less risky enterprise. Unwillingness to report crime to the police or to intervene in a crime, both of which result from fear of crime, also reduces risk to the offender. The effects of the fear of crime can thus contribute to the crime problem. What is to be done?

The most critical need is for social policies that will effectively reduce the need and desire to commit robbery. Full employment, economic security for all citizens, realistic economic expectations, the elimination of racial discrimination, and the solution of the heroin problem will all have many benefits, one of which would be the reduction of robbery and the diminished suffering of the elderly through this crime.

Closer interpersonal relations, more frequent social interaction, and stronger social bonds might also make the streets safer. Policies oriented toward such goals—such as incentives for businessmen to keep their establishments open after dark, well-lit parks, institutionalized means for people to meet each other, and more carefully designed buildings—might strengthen the fabric of community life, enhance informal social control, and reduce the risk of victimization.

References

Conklin, John E. 1975. *The Impact of Crime.* New York: Macmillan Inc.

_____ . 1972. *Robbery and the Criminal Justice System.* Philadelphia: J.B. Lippincott Company.

Curtis, Lynn A. 1974. *Criminal Violence: National Patterns and Behavior.* Lexington, Massachusetts: Lexington Books, D.C. Heath and Company.

Feagin, Joe R. 1970. "Home-Defense and the Police: Black and White Perspectives," *American Behavioral Scientist* XIII (May), 797-814.

Furstenberg, Frank F., Jr. 1972. "Fear of Crime and Its Effects on Citizen Behavior." Paper presented at the Symposium on Studies of Public Experience, Knowledge and Opinion of Crime and Justice. Bureau of Social Science Research, Inc. Washington, D.C., March.

Marx, Gary T., and Dane Archer. 1972. "Picking up the Gun: Some Organizational and Survey Data on Community Police Patrols." Paper presented at the Symposium on Studies of Public Experience, Knowledge and Opinion of Crime and Justice. Bureau of Social Science Research, Inc. Washington, D.C., March.

11 A Service Model for Elderly Crime Victims

David M. Friedman

Crime and fear of crime are the priority issues for millions of elderly citizens. A recent *New York Times* survey showed that crime is the major preoccupation of 71 percent of New Yorkers aged 65 and over. Each year thousands of crimes are committed against older citizens; and although millions of dollars are spent to process and rehabilitate the perpetrators of these crimes, little is done to assist the elderly victim.

According to police statistics in New York City, for the first 11 months of 1974, women over age 65 accounted for 15 percent of homicide victims—a number far out of proportion to their percentage of the population. These reported crime rates, however, must be used in conjunction with other indicators to judge the actual level of victimization of the aged. The truth is that many serious crimes against the elderly are never reported to the police, and those hoping to address the crime issue can no longer ignore this fact.

The Problem

Why are elderly women and men so often targets for violent attack and robbery? In order to propose realistic programs that can help them reduce their vulnerability, we must identify those factors that increase the susceptibility of the elderly to attack. Those factors most important are:

1. Many older people live alone.
2. Many are in poor health, and an older person too weak to run away or resist is a prime target for attack.
3. Many of our elderly live on fixed incomes, which restrict them to residing in low-income neighborhoods where crime levels are high.
4. Many older New York City citizens are in rent-controlled apartments and are unable to find and afford comparable living quarters in safer neighborhoods.
5. Finally, many aging citizens are reluctant to report crimes against themselves for fear of reprisals. Their fear leads to reluctance to go to the police and makes them particularly vulnerable to revictimization.

What happens to the life-style of an elderly victim who has been attacked or lives in constant fear of attack and theft?

1. People living on fixed incomes provided by social security or pensions suffer serious loss at the theft of even a small amount of money; and the procedures for recovering or being reimbursed for stolen social security funds are cumbersome and inadequate for meeting the crisis that results from theft. The replacement of a stolen TV, which for many older people is their primary diversion and companion, also causes severe financial hardship. The theft of a TV also has serious consequences in terms of the socialization difficulties of older people as well.

2. Physically, many old people never recover from the effects of a beating or violent attack. Recuperative abilities decline with age and an injury that heals in a younger person often remains a life-long ailment for an elderly person.

3. Emotionally, the feelings of isolation often experienced by many elderly poor are compounded by the terror they constantly feel after they have been attacked.

4. Finally, fear of attack or trauma caused by attack leads many older people to drastically curtail their contacts with the world outside their apartments and to modify their daily habits. Many senior citizen programs go underused because of this fear, and thousands of the elderly confine themselves to their apartments after 3:00 P.M., when school children are on the streets.

Proposed Plan

In light of the problems outlined in the first section of this discussion, what is a viable course of action with which to address the problems of crime and the elderly? I offer a model based on a pilot program to service victims of violent crimes in the Bronx. The Crime Victims Service Center was the first government-sponsored service program in the United States that assists victims of violent crimes. The program is funded by a grant from the Law Enforcement Assistance Administration to the mayor's Criminal Justice Coordinating Council of New York City. The Center for the Study of Social Intervention, Department of Psychiatry of Albert Einstein College of Medicine, is administering it in the Bronx.

Our specific mandate is not limited to servicing elderly crime victims, but for the first seven months of operation of the Crime Victims Service Center, people 60 and over represented 11 percent of the cases serviced by our project staff out of 160+ cases. A breakdown by crime code of the elderly cases serviced shows that clients over 60 accounted for 14.3 percent of the homicide cases and 30.4 percent of the robbery cases we serviced. A high percentage of white clients over 60 is evident when it is noted that they represented 33.3 percent of all white clients serviced, but only 4.6 percent of all black clients, and 3.8 percent of Hispanic clients serviced are in the elderly group. Of the total number of clients over 60 serviced (11 percent of the total), the white elderly accounted for

70.6 percent, the black elderly 17.6 percent, and the Hispanic elderly 11.8 percent. The racial breakdown for all clients serviced was 23.4 percent white, 42.2 percent black, and 33.8 percent Hispanic.

Several hypotheses could explain the high concentration of white elderly victims in the white client group using the services of our center. One reason may be that many of the elderly whites whom we service live in neighborhoods where the racial balance has shifted, and crime rates are higher than where more affluent, younger white residents live; and living within the bounds of a fixed income does not offer many opportunities for moving away from a neighborhood. The fact is that in New York City many of the elderly reside in rent-controlled apartments and cannot move because in so doing they are subject to new rent laws under which their rents are drastically increased. There are also many elderly whites who choose to remain in the neighborhoods where they have lived for years although the areas have deteriorated and are crime ridden. Often, fear of the unknown is greater than fear of what a person already knows, and many people are unwilling to leave homes in which they have lived to raise families. Memories are sometimes impossible to leave.

Another point that may explain the high level of white-elderly victimization is the fact that their physical and social isolation may be greater than that of blacks and Hispanics. In the South Bronx, at least, many elderly blacks and Hispanics are part of extended families. They often live with their families and help mothers raise the children where the father is absent.

Finally, a third factor that may explain the higher proportion of white elderly victims in the Bronx is racial hostility. This is especially evident in violent attacks by youths where racial comments are made to the elderly white victim. Many of these attacks involve outrageous physical brutality where profit is not the motive and the elderly victim offers no resistance.

So far, statistics on the citywide racial makeup of the elderly-victim group have not been systematically analyzed. It may be said, however, for all the reasons mentioned above, that elderly whites are victimized far more than other white victims, and for this reason, a program to help elderly crime victims would probably tend to provide services to a greater proportion of white crime victims.

Model Components

The following is a brief description of the components of a program that might address the problem of crime and the elderly. The first element of the program would be the human service component to include both direct and referral services.

Direct service would use trained counselors to provide counseling to reduce the intensity of emotional problems that follow an attack. This sort of immediate crisis intervention following a violent crime can do much to help the person cope with his or her fears and anxieties, which might otherwise linger for years. A counselor may help the victim to deal with the feeling of personal guilt. Following a crime, the victim will often blame himself for going out at the wrong time or for not checking to see whether anyone is in the hall. Without proper and timely intervention, these guilt feelings may reinforce further withdrawal into the relative safety of a shut-in life.

The human service component could serve as a mechanism for linking elderly crime victims with appropriate existing community services. Specific advocacy procedures could be developed with agencies, including a crime victims compensation program, should one exist, social security, local mental health clinics, hospitals, home-maker services, and the other services available to senior citizens. The crime victim counselors would assist elderly victims by acting as community facilitators and as expeditors, connecting victims with the appropriate services; and the crime victim program could develop preferential attention as well as more adequate procedures for securing services for elderly crime victims.

Service Needs

The following cases demonstrate the need for direct and referral services to elderly victims. An 83-year-old woman's husband was murdered by four youths in the hallway of their apartment house in the Bronx. We were called by police and were asked to see her. Severe signs of emotional trauma were evident while interviewing her. Following the violent death of her husband she stopped eating and began to vomit and complain of abdominal pains. She was unable to sleep at night and was extremely agitated. Quickly her mental health deteriorated to the point where she developed a speech impediment, was unable to sleep, and had a generalized tremor of the hands and feet. We referred her to an affiliated hospital psychiatric program for therapy that would deal with her problems. She was put on Thorazine and improved, but the drug treatment was discontinued because of an allergic reaction. Her mental anxieties appear to be diminishing following a series of therapy sessions.

We have other cases that demonstrate the need for new procedures to help replace stolen social security checks. Presently, in New York City, if a social security check is stolen during a mugging, the victim must wait until the check clears in Birmingham, Alabama before it can be replaced—this can take anywhere from two to six months. If the check had been cashed by the victim prior to the mugging and his money stolen, he would be referred to an emergency procedure for public assistance for funds. The discrepancy between services in these two cases defies logic, and the crime victims program should act as advocates to facilitate emergency check-replacement procedures.

Another victim-related service often requested is help in securing a new

Medicare card, once it is stolen. Help can also be given to the elderly in applying for financial compensation under the New York State Crime Victims Compensation Board program. Under the present legislation there is a definite bias against the elderly's eligibility for compensation. In order to qualify for compensation under New York State law, one must have out of pocket expenses for medical or other services of at least $100 unreimbursed from other sources, or have loss of earnings for at least two continuous weeks. Since most senior citizens are retired and are on social security and Medicare, they are usually ineligible to apply under the law as it now reads. Up to $1,500 is available to cover burial costs if conditions of severe financial hardship are met.

The following service we provided another elderly client points up another type of problem. A 70-year-old woman's husband was murdered. A few months afterward several individuals were apprehended in another murder and confessed to the murder of her husband. His body, however, had been disposed of in a city dump, and the police reported it would be too costly to exhume it. Murder charges could not be made since the body was unavailable. What the woman actually cared about was seeing that her husband's murderers were punished. Since they had been apprehended on another charge, she wished to be informed of the events in the upcoming trial. Our role was to contact the district attorney prosecuting the case to insure that the woman was notified of the status of the trial. We located him and explained the situation. He agreed to keep the woman informed, and this information has helped reduce her anxiety and is providing her with hope that her husband's killers will be brought to justice. Parenthetically, since her husband's body was never recovered, no claim could be filed for burial reimbursement with the New York State Compensation Board.

Any service offered in a victim program must do more than provide information on where to secure help. In any large city, and especially in New York, a "road map" of available services serves little purpose. The elderly victim in his or her time of need is often unable to find the way through the jungle of social service programs and agencies. A trained staff of enablers and facilitators is needed—people who can assist the elderly by acting in their behalf before all the various agencies and by pursuing comprehensive follow-up, which is often the most important part of *any* service referral program.

The second element of an elderly-victim program must be a prevention component. Information on personal safety and on security devices should be distributed to the elderly, but great care must be taken not to place too heavy an emphasis on the effect that individual elderly citizens or senior citizen groups can have in preventing crime. The police have developed sophisticated multimedia crime prevention presentations; however there is little evidence to support the effectiveness of many of the suggested techniques. I do not want to imply that crime prevention efforts by elderly individuals and groups cannot help; but I am suggesting that too much emphasis is being placed on this concept by the police. In certain extreme cases the police appear to blame crime victims for their misfortune because endorsed crime prevention methods are not followed. The real responsibility for protecting the aging still remains with local law enforcement officials.

New and innovative efforts must be made to develop effective crime prevention programs for the elderly. Self-help programs such as tenant patrols and instruction in self-defense do not appear to be suitable for senior citizens. Perhaps door-to-door escort services providing protection during shopping trips, and elevator operators employed to escort the elderly from the elevator to the safety of their apartments are the kinds of service most needed to safeguard older people. One of the most frequent forms of attack against the elderly in the Bronx comes from youngsters who hide and wait for the elderly to open their doors when they return home. The young assailants then rush the elderly person, pushing him or her inside the apartment and often injure the person. The police call this tactic "robbing the cradle" because it is as simple as taking candy from a baby. New techniques of crime require new techniques of crime prevention. An elderly crime-victim project in close contact with the victim can use its resources to develop such new techniques.

An essential component of an elderly crime victim program is that of assuming an advocacy role—identify problems; develop alternative statutes, rules, ordinances and legislation; recommend them to appropriate legislative bodies, individuals or organizations; select test cases and litigate issues involving the rights of elderly victims. I have already noted the inadequacies of procedures for replacing stolen social security checks and of eligibility requirements for help from the New York State Crime Victims Compensation Board. In order to service elderly victims effectively, an advocacy component would work to change these procedures and others that hinder aiding the aged.

Advocacy activities can press local, state, and federal programs and politicians to work changes on existing procedures and regulations so they more effectively serve the needs of elderly crime victims. Advocates could also work with a local chapter of the American Institute of Architects in developing physical design concepts to be implemented in the construction of housing for the elderly—perhaps placing corridors on the exterior of apartment houses where they are highly visible—then security might be better. Advocate activities can also be effective in changing existing laws. Currently under New York State law, a minor (under 16) gets a maximum of 18 months for even the most serious crimes—including murder. Since many aging citizens are the targets of violent attacks by minors, an advocacy position could be developed concerning changes in sentencing.

Another advocacy activity that might be pursued is the development of a credit card system for the aged to eliminate the need for carrying cash or social security checks and thus eliminate the stolen funds and checks problem. Credit cards would be issued to each individual and social security funds deposited into each person's account monthly. Senior citizens would no longer need to be theft victims when the social security check arrives; and computer technology already in use by banks and credit card companies would make implementation of such a program immediately practical.

Component Interdependence

I have described the skeleton structure of a service model for elderly crime victims. I want to emphasize that components of the model are interdependent. It is our feeling that implementation of any single component, in or by itself, is insufficient unless combined with the other two. Our experience in establishing the Crime Victim Service Program illustrates this interdependence.

During the first year of implementation, the program consisted solely of a human service component. We feel strongly that this limitation was an important reason why the services offered by the program were greatly underused—given the normal problems encountered in initiating a new project. Greater use of the human service component occurred only after advocacy and preventive activities occurred. The conclusion we draw from this experience is that a service component in or of itself is not sufficient unless it is combined with advocacy and preventive activities.

Service Gaps

As to service gaps that legitimately could and should be addressed, the Crime Victims Service Center has succeeded in identifying at least three—protection, legal services, and immediate financial assistance to crime victims. Although these problems are those of many other groups of people, the elderly experience them with more difficulty than most.

1. Law enforcement officials are incapable of providing adequate protection to victims who have been threatened—many older citizens are aware of this and either do not report crimes or never press charges.

2. Affordable and adequate legal service is another necessity the elderly poor lack, although legal aid programs are always available to needy offenders. The district attorney represents the people of the state of New York in criminal cases, not the victim personally. His concern with clearing the calendar and processing cases is not often coincidental with the victim's best interest. Neglect of the victim's legal rights riddles the entire criminal justice system. The Constitution has been applied to safeguarding the rights of offenders, but little has yet been done to protect the rights of victims. There is provision for personal representation on behalf of defendants, but the same is not provided victims. If the district attorney's office would counterbalance the free legal representation of defendants with similar service and concern for the victims rights, more people would report crimes and press charges.

3. Immediate emergency financial assistance is the third gap we have identified. Agency procedures are currently so involved and cumbersome that immediate emergency financial aid is simply not available. Unfortunately, for an elderly person who has been mugged and robbed, his needs are often immediate and "emergency" financial assistance arriving in three days, a week, or more might be too late.

Each of these three issues raises issues around which advocacy activities can be seriously addressed to effectively serve the needs of elderly crime victims.

Conclusion

I conclude with the hope that the thoughts presented in this discussion will lead to further refinement of the ideas presented and to the implementation of active programs that will address the problems of the elderly crime victim. Although it is true that crime rates reflect broad societal conditions and ailments, expedient programs are needed to address the critical situation that exists. The luxury of long-term programs to change societal conditions and attitudes must be subservient to the need for programs that will insure the safety and security of our elderly. Victims of violent crime are generally neglected. The elderly victims are twice victimized—once by the perpetrator and second by virtue of their being elderly and treated almost as second-class citizens.

We must put careful thought and planning into the development of new programs. We must pay attention to the needs and attitudes of the elderly. Behavior patterns and habits that have developed over many years are not easily amended, and new services may go unused by those whose established patterns of daily living do not coincide with proposed ideas. We must consult the elderly and solicit their participation in planning effective programs so that we insure the suitability of services to the needs and attitudes of older people.

**Part III
The Criminal Justice System
and the Elderly Victim**

12 Purse Snatch: Robbery's Ugly Stepchild

James B. Richardson

The crime of purse snatch is one of the most serious and neglected of all crimes. Perpetrated primarily against elderly women, it can cause hardship far beyond the often minimal value of the contents of the purse. Over 30 percent (30%) of the 1974 purse snatches in Portland, Oregon resulted in some kind of injury to the victim. Almost 10 percent (10%) of all 1974 purse snatches resulted in injuries serious enough to require hospitalization or other emergency medical treatment. Almost 60 percent (60%) of all the victims were over 50. The older the victim, the more likely she is to be injured and the more likely the injury is to be serious. More than half of the injuries in the over-60 age bracket were of a serious nature. For many elderly victims, a purse snatch can mean being crippled for the rest of their lives.

The purpose of this chapter is to draw attention to the serious nature of the crime and to focus some attention on the problems faced by law enforcement agencies in dealing with purse snatches. Because each jurisdiction will have its own level of purse snatch activity, the main import of this study must be to encourage each agency to look more closely at purse snatches and to stimulate new programs to reduce its tragic effects.

Victims

Purse snatch victims present a homogeneous group whose common elements go beyond sex and age. (See Table 12-1.) Often long-time residents of transitional and deteriorating neighborhoods, these victims live alienated from their surroundings. Threatened by the unfamiliar changes in their environment, the elderly often have difficulty establishing protective friendships with their new neighbors.

Elderly women living alone often are forced to patterns of behavior most likely to make them victims of purse snatches. Most purse snatches occur while victims are going to or from the store or are walking to, waiting for, or walking from public transportation. The poor, and especially the elderly poor, are particularly dependent on shopping habits and travel methods that place them in the most likely positions to become victims.

Since the purse snatcher usually approaches from behind at a fast run, positive identification is very difficult. But even where identification can be made, victims often express fear of reprisals and a general reluctance to place further burdens on their position in the neighborhood.

121

Table 12-1
Victims by Age and Race

Age/Race	White	Black	Other/Unknown
Under 20	18	3	0
20-29	39	1	2
30-39	19	0	0
40-49	26	2	0
50-59	34	1	0
60-69	45	0	0
70+	67	1	0

$N = 258$.

Suspects

Because of some of the reasons cited above, accurate data on suspects is not always available. From suspect descriptions by victims, however, some general comments can be made. Perhaps the most significant descriptor of the purse snatcher is youth. Over 70 percent of purse snatchers are described as being under 18 years of age. Because of the wide discrepancy in ages between the victim and the suspect, accurate age estimates and descriptions are very hard to obtain. Race differences between suspect and victim further compound the identification problem.

The fact that juveniles compose the majority of offenders also tends to reinforce the attitude of the public that the crime is not serious. Coupled with the different treatment given juveniles in the court and rehabilitation process, this aspect of the suspect profile often prompts law enforcement officers to indulge in their frustration through inattention to purse snatch crimes. (Please refer to Table 12-2.)

Identifying the Extent of Purse Snatches

Certainly one of the problems of dealing with the crime of purse snatch is that no clear picture of its extent is available from normal crime classification procedures. To avoid duplicate and costly crime data collection most major police departments follow the Federal Bureau of Investigation's Uniform Crime Report classification system. The crime of purse snatch is classified (depending on the amount of force used) as either a larceny (usually under $50) or an unarmed robbery. Thus, the police have no readily available indicators to draw upon for information about purse snatches. To confound matters, purse snatches may fall under state law as either a felony or a misdemeanor, although the

Table 12-2
Suspects by Age and Race

Age/Race	White	Black	Other/Unknown
Under 10	0	5	0
10-19	91	143	2
20-29	20	32	2
30-39	2	7	1
40+	1	0	0

N = 306.
Note: Crimes in which suspect descriptions did not include sex and race descriptions are excluded on this table.

method and intent of the perpetrator are the same. As in some other crimes, criminals are prosecuted more on the luck or misfortune of their victims than on the nature of their acts.

As a result of all of the above police response to purse snatches has been, at best, lukewarm. Cognizant of the unlikelihood of sanctions, even if an identification, arrest, and conviction could be made, most police officers become disenchanted with enforcement measures against purse snatchers. The magnitude of the crime is often hidden from the street officer in that prime time for purse snatching often overlaps shifts and/or patrol boundaries. Even though the likelihood of serious injury and the cost to the victim is greater on the average in purse snatches, both commercial and pedestrian holdups are viewed as more serious crimes. (Please see Table 12-3.) Perhaps this is because the potential for serious harm is perceived as greater in an armed as opposed to unarmed robbery. The suspects are generally viewed as more serious criminals, and often have records to support this contention. Because of this, police officers often view armed robberies as a more "prestigious" crime to work against than purse snatch.

Cost to the victim presents another picture, however. Although the immediate cost, in terms of property taken, is greater in an armed holdup of a commercial establishment, the average victim cost is higher in purse snatches. The burden of paying for these crimes falls on different shoulders. The commercial establishment can internalize its costs and pass them onto its customers in the form of higher prices. Since a majority of commercial robbery victims are convenience-oriented establishments open into the late evening, this increase in cost can be viewed as the price of special service. Victims of pedestrian holdups and purse snatches can usually only internalize the immediate costs, that is, loss of property. When personal injury results, as often is the case in purse snatches involving elderly women, medical costs can be quite extensive. The costs, most often through Medicare and Medicaid, are external-

Table 12-3
Percent of Injuries by Robbery Subcategories

Crime	Commercial Robbery	Pedestrian Robbery	Robbery (Purse Snatch)
Percentage of Total Robberies	44% (712)	46% (794)	13% (228)
Percentage of Injuries per Subcategory	4% (32)	33% (262)	44% (101)

N = 1,734.
Note: An injury includes any contusion, abrasion, or other physical trauma not necessarily requiring medical attention. The purse snatch subcategory does not include 414 purse snatches classified as larcenies.

ized, that is, paid for by those with no direct relationship with the victim. The remoteness of those paying for the crime of purse snatch from those victimized further diminishes the likelihood that the problem will be identified as serious and that timely, corrective measures will be taken. In commercial robberies store owners can form a very vocal lobby to protect their own pecuniary interst. No such counterpart is apparent for purse snatching or pedestrian holdups. Furthermore, the cost of purse snatch is not readily available. These costs may appear much later in the form of months or even years of recurring medical bills, hospitalization, and incidental costs that are all but impossible to trace.

Programs in Portland, Oregon

As an impact city, Portland is receiving funds to reduce burglaries and stranger-to-stranger street crimes. Part of this money supports a small Crime Analysis Unit that is given the responsibility of identifying specific crime trends and patterns. Purse snatch is one crime given constant attention.

Throughout the period of this program various methods of suppression and apprehension have been tried, ranging from uniformed patrol to decoys. Suppression effects have been attained with both "covert" and uniform patrol. However, apprehensions have been few and residual effects minimal. Those that have been made have been the result of covert patrol in high incident areas. Decoy strategies have been unsuccessful.

Recently, much effort has been given to identifying seasonal and other predictive variables and identifying specific geographic problem areas. When periods of high purse snatch are anticipated, such as just before Christmas, special attention is given by means of media spots reminding potential victims, notices to patrol officers, dissemination of brochures, and the like. As of May 1,

1975 purse snatch figures were running 26 percent below last year. However, the real test of our program effectiveness will come in November [1975] when purse snatches are expected to increase dramatically.

Currently, the Portland Police Bureau is taking a close look at the economics of all robbery crimes, not only from the standpoint of police costs, but also from the viewpoint of victim costs.

What Can Law Enforcement Agencies Do?

1. We can educate the victim. Multimedia awareness programs can be planned for those times of the year when purse snatch crimes are expected to be highest. Officers can courteously warn potential victims, on the street or at bus stops, against being alone or carrying a purse during the periods when most purse snatches occur. Brochures can be distributed at grocery stores and shopping centers.

2. Patrol officers should be particularly watchful for potential victims in high purse snatch areas. Known purse snatchers or suspicious suspects fitting a purse snatcher's profile can be identified and a field contact report filled out.

3. New deterrence and apprehension strategies should be tried and evaluated to determine which works best.

4. Law enforcement agencies can appraise juvenile authorities of the seriousness of the crime and the necessity for their active participation in deterrence.

5. Arrangements can often be made through service organizations to escort elderly women on foot to and from shopping centers or to provide transportation. Thought should be given to restitution on the part of convicted purse snatchers to victims by providing escort service.

6. Through crime analysis law enforcement agencies can look beyond the artificial classification criteria of the Uniform Crime Reports and fully identify the extent of purse snatch crimes in their jurisdiction.

Conclusion

The reduction of purse snatch crimes depends upon the accomplishments of many difficult tasks. The public must be made aware of the seriousness of the crime. The potential victim must be convinced to change long established shopping and dressing habits. Sanctions must be found to deter potential purse snatchers and the police must be persuaded that their efforts will be effective. Progress can be achieved. Diligence must be maintained.

13

The Urban Police Function in Regard to the Elderly: A Special Case of Police Community Relations

Richard E. Sykes

At the present time there is a social movement that seeks to single out crimes against the elderly as an especially serious aspect of the general increase in crime. In part this is due to the organization of senior citizens, who, as they become an increasingly large proportion of the population, become a more effective political force. The movement also has its roots in the revulsion felt by all at victimizing those least able to defend themselves, and economically least able to afford the costs of victimization.

Older persons, especially elderly women, are particularly vulnerable to street crimes because of their inability to defend themselves against much younger and stronger males, and because they may be injured more easily. They may also be psychologically less resilient, so that the trauma of a purse snatching or even burglary has greater effects. Senior citizens have very limited incomes so that loss of a small amount of money or burglary of a television set seriously limits their life-style. Since many elderly civilians live in high crime rate sections of the city, they may be more at risk than other sectors of the population.

The number of studies of the relation of the elderly and crime is not voluminous. Historically some dealt with the elderly violator.[1] Recently some attention was given to the elderly victim, both in terms of crimes known to police, and victimization.[2] These studies demonstrated that there were certain crimes of which the elderly were more likely to be victims, notably personal larceny with contact, but generally did not show that the elderly suffered any more from crime than other age groups.

Crimes known to police are those deemed serious enough by either the complainant or the officer to become a matter of official record. Victimization data, on the other hand, include many instances where no request was made for police service. Much police work involves contacts with civilians that are not officially recorded. Officers may have judged that what a civilian considered a criminal victimization was not in fact a crime or so minor as to make a report unjustified.[3] Many police contacts with civilians are not related to crime at all from either a police or a civilian perspective, but with the serious personal crises of civilians. Thus Phyllis Mensh Brostoff, Roberta Brown, and Robert Butler reported that as a result of *Project Assist*, 220 elderly persons received direct help such as "emergency money, replacement of food stamps, medical assistance, and sheltered care."[4]

This research was supported by Grant 5 RO1 MH23144-02, "Comparative Quantitative Studies of Police-Citizen Encounters," from the U.S. Public Health Service, National Institute of Mental Health, Center for Studies of Crime and Delinquency.

127

If the urban police function in regard to the elderly is to be understood, it is necessary to know (1) whether the elderly are at risk more than the general population, and (2) what the nature of the actual consumption pattern by the elderly of police services is, since this likely differs from both crimes officially known to police and victimization data. Departmental policy should be made in the light of improved knowledge of what sectors of the populations are at greater risk, as well as of public consumption patterns.

In order to provide some information pertinent to these questions a data base of 4,918 police-civilian encounters observed by scientists in two major American cities was analyzed. Three questions were asked: (1) Are police contacts with the elderly more frequent than would be expected given their proportion of the population? (2) What is the nature of police contacts with the elderly? (3) Are police contacts with the elderly different from those with the nonelderly?

If the elderly constitute a high-risk segment of the population, they should be disproportionately represented as complainants. If the elderly are especially vulnerable to street crime, they should be more likely to come into contact with police in public places. If criminal victimization is the main reason for police contact with the elderly, they should be overrepresented in this category, and underrepresented in other categories of police contact.

Data Collection

Observers rode with the police in two cities with a combined central city population of about 750,000 systematically coding the reason for each encounter; its location; classifying the content and the emotional tone of each statement by officer or civilian; noting acts of special salience, such as violence; the types of information on which the officer's ultimate decision was based; the outcome of the encounter, as well as many other variables relevant either to police and the law, or to the social psychological understanding of these events including demographic characteristics of the civilians involved. The data constitute a random shift sample of police activities and, based on comparison with other large-scale observational studies, such as those of A. Reiss and of D. Cruse and J. Rubin appear to reflect in most ways the general nature of urban police activities throughout the United States.[5]

Data Analysis

Overall Contact with Police

Fourteen percent of the population of the two cities were over 65 according to the 1970 Census. Of 4,918 encounters, 996 involved activities in which no civilian participated (silent alarms, for instance) or else were resolved or not evident when the police arrived. Of the remaining 3,922 encounters, 343 or approximately 9 percent involved an elderly civilian in the role of complainant, suspect, participant, or bystander. Overall, elderly civilians were somewhat underrepresented in their contacts with police.

Initiation

It is now well known, though contrary to the popular stereotype, that most uniformed police patrol activity is in response to consumer, that is, civilian complainant demand.[6] Most encounters are reactive, not proactive from the police point of view. Our data show that this was even more true of elderly civilians than of the nonelderly. If motor vehicle violations are not included, police initiated contact with the elderly about half as much as with other age groups. About 5 percent of their contacts with the elderly were proactive. The contrast was even more marked if motor vehicle stops were included. The ordinary citizen's typical contact with police is related to a motor vehicle offense, and such offenses may consist of up to one-sixth of police contacts with civilians, but our data show that an elderly driver was about one fourth as likely to be stopped as one who was nonelderly. It therefore appears that even more than with civilians generally, if police deal with the elderly, it is very likely to be in response to requests by the elderly themselves.

Type of Activity

The reasons for police contact with the elderly were significantly different from those that bring them together with the nonelderly. We divided police activities into five broad categories: alleged crimes against person or property; alleged breaches of public order; pure service or emergency medical assistance unrelated to crime; alleged motor vehicle violations; and calls that involved suspicions which turned out to be unfounded, or which were resolved or in which the suspected civilians dispersed before the officers arrived or in which no civilians were involved. From Table 13-1 it is evident that officers had about the same or proportionately fewer contacts with elderly civilians in all but two of these categories. The one important exception was pure service. Elderly civilians sought noncrime-related service from police about twice as much as was expected. The percent of crime-related encounters was slightly larger than expected, but not startling.

A closer inspection of the nature of these activities shows that although the elderly did not suffer from crimes against the person more than others, they did suffer more than their share of personal larcenies with contact, no doubt due to their physical vulnerability. This was a very small proportion of elderly

Table 13-1

Actual and Expected Percentage of Police Contact with the Elderly by Type of Activity

Type of Activity	Actual Percent	Expected Percent
Crime	32	26
Order	26	25
Service	25	14
Traffic	6	27
Other	11	9
Total	100	101

$N = 343$.
$X^2 = 92.37$.
4 d.f.
$p < 0.001$.

victimizations. Primarily they were victims of other crimes against property, especially burglaries, which constituted 90 percent of their criminal victimizations. In the area of order maintenance it appears that the elderly complained disproportionately more of minor harassment especially by the young. Children and adolescents, more often than not neighbors, caused senior citizens to seek police intervention to remedy a wide variety of trespasses and annoyances.

Location of Activity

Although the elderly are disproportionately victims of street crimes, as I have already indicated, they were not large in number compared to the number of burglaries. Perhaps for this reason police were about twice as likely to contact an elderly as opposed to a nonelderly civilian in a private place such as a home or apartment. Even so, as with the public generally, police and the elderly usually had contact in public (see Table 13-2).

Quality of Interaction

Interaction between officers and senior citizens was not significantly different from that between officers and the nonelderly. Both had a tendency to reciprocate disrespect and hostility.[a] An elderly civilian was a little more likely

[a]For a theory of the relation between police and civilian disrespect see R. Sykes and J. Clark, "A Theory of Deference Exchange in Police-Civilian Encounters," *American Journal of Sociology*, 81 (November, 1975).

Table 13-2
Actual and Expected Percentage of Police Contact with the Elderly by Location

Type of Location	Actual Percent	Expected Percent
Private house	21.6	9.8
Apartment	12.0	6.7
Business	5.0	6.0
Public place	61.5	77.6
Total	100.1	100.1

$N = 343.$
$X^2 = 66.46.$
3 d.f.
$p < 0.001.$

to get away with unilateral disrespect to the officer. Officers were also somewhat less apt to resort to direct verbal control over the elderly, suggesting that either the elderly needed less control, or else that officers dealt with them more diplomatically. But there were differences in regard to particular kinds of calls. Officers were less patient in encounters with elderly civilians pertaining to public order, perhaps because in some cases they view the elderly as overly particular (see Table 13-3). In encounters dealing with public order this impatience was reciprocated by the elderly, but the elderly also tended to be more disrespectful to officers than most civilians in encounters dealing with either crime or traffic (see Table 13-4). The picture that emerges is one in which the oldster succeeded in being just a bit more crotchety than the officer, not an easy accomplishment. But these differences were not great, and are not essentially important.

Role Structure

Obviously the elderly are much more likely to be complainants than suspects. Whereas 10 percent of all complainants were elderly, only 3 percent of all suspects were elderly. Since 14 percent of the population is over 65, the elderly were underrepresented even as complainants. A less obvious finding is that elderly complainants were no more apt to be alone than young complainants. In fact, almost the reverse was true. An elderly complainant was somewhat more apt to have a companion than a young one. Half of the encounters involving the elderly included an elderly complainant. Only 11 percent included an elderly violator and in most cases the violator was alone. In about 35 percent of encounters involving the elderly, the elderly appeared as participants in the interaction, but not in the leading role of suspect or complainant.

Table 13-3

Actual and Expected Percentage of Police Hostility to the Elderly by Activity

Type of Activity	Hostility	
	Percent Observed	Percent Expected
Crime	10	9
Order	28	19
Service	7	8
Traffic	21	19
Other	8	9

$N = 343$.

Note: For purposes of this table an encounter is included if one or more statements by the officer was hostile.

Table 13-4

Actual and Expected Percentage of Elderly Civilian Hostility to the Police by Activity

Type of Activity	Hostility	
	Percent Observed	Percent Expected
Crime	12	8
Order	23	17
Service	7	7
Traffic	18	10
Other	8	7

$N = 343$.

Note: For purposes of this table an encounter is included if one or more statements by the elderly civilian were hostile.

Encounter Outcome

Outcomes of encounters involving the elderly differed from others primarily in regard to tickets and reports. Proportionately about the same percent of encounters involving the elderly ended in arrest, or in negotiated solutions short of arrest. Because the elderly were stopped for traffic violations much less often they received proportionately fewer tickets. On the other hand an official report was requested and made nearly twice as often. Because the elderly were about twice as likely to request that an official report be made official police statistics are likely to reflect this difference in complainant preference (about 7 percent make such requests generally, but about 14 percent among the elderly). This suggests that crimes known to police may overemphasize elderly victimization as compared to other age groups.

Other Factors

Encounters involving the elderly were much less apt to be all male (26 percent as opposed to 50 percent generally). They were slightly more apt to include working class civilians (70 percent as opposed to 65 percent). Encounters involving an elderly person were just as likely to include someone who had been drinking (about 20 percent of the total number of activities).

In our research we tried to judge whether a crime had actually occurred and, if so, whether it was within the police power. Our data show that the elderly were more likely to have actually suffered a felony than the nonelderly (17.4 percent to 11.4 percent), but were less likely to have been the victim of a misdemeanor (21 percent to 27 percent). With the elderly, officers were less able to do something about the victimization, other than take a report. Officers could actually act only about 13 percent of the time with elderly victims, but 20 percent of the time with nonelderly victims. Although the outcomes in all cases were usually unilaterally imposed by the officers, about twice as many nonarrest outcomes of encounters in which the elderly were participants involved mutual negotiation between them and the officer than between the nonelderly and officers (16 percent to 8 percent).

Discussion

These data are not very dramatic, but in their implications for the urban police function in regard to the elderly they are quite important. They suggest that the elderly are not really so unusual after all insofar as police are concerned, and that for this very reason the problem of responding to their needs in many ways is not so different from responding to the needs of the average citizen. But this does not mean there is no problem of police response. Let us start by summarizing what we know about the urban uniformed police patrol function generally, and make appropriate modifications where necessary in regard to senior citizens.

1. Police are virtually the only public service agency available to citizens 24 hours a day, 365 days a year.

2. Police are virtually the only public agency or helping profession that makes house calls in response to consumer demand. This is more true of their service to the elderly than the nonelderly.

3. Police are a multipurpose agency, and concern with criminal violations occupies a minority of their time, at least insofar as uniformed patrol officers are concerned. Combined requests for the maintenance of order and for service are more frequent consumer demands.[b]

[b]Many writers have commented on this tendency. One classic study is E. Cumming et al., "Policeman as Philosopher, Guide and Friend," *Social Problems*, 12 (Winter, 1965), pp. 276-286.

4. Police are a consumer-oriented agency. They perform their activities in response to specific requests by particular citizens. This is even more true of the elderly than the nonelderly.

5. Police generally and unavoidably arrive at the scene after the fact, especially in cases of alleged criminal violations of a serious nature. Although the response capability of police fulfills a kind of general deterrence function, in actual fact most property violations occur within private space inaccessible to police except by invitation, and usually when the occupant is absent.[7] Even in the case of street crime, short of posting an officer on every corner, the likelihood of an officer being present when the crime occurs is very slim. His presence is demanded after the fact. This is more true with the elderly than with the nonelderly. The officer is less likely to have the power to apprehend the violator and more likely to be reduced to making out a report. His role is more akin to that of bureaucratic record keeper.

These facts of life insofar as the police function is concerned are not likely to please those with a traditional law and order image of police or extravagant hopes for change. The police relationship to the elderly has many possibilities, but also limitations. The ability of the police to cut down the rate of crime against the elderly using traditional means is not very great. Not only this, but since the elderly do not in fact constitute an especially high-risk group, although they are certainly in some ways an especially vulnerable group, it is doubtful whether extensive investments in programs aimed only at the elderly and that use traditional means of prevention or response are justified.

Nor does it seem necessary to use elaborate theoretical explanations of these data. Considered as an entire group the elderly are underrepresented in police encounters because they are much less apt to commit violations of the law or of the peace or of traffic regulations, or at least to have been so labeled. As complainants, although not quite proportionately represented, this may not be so surprising since many of the elderly are sufficiently disabled to be virtually confined either to their own homes, or to segregated facilities for the sick and dependent, and so not to be a risk. It seems likely that it is what might be termed the "able-bodied elderly" who are more at risk, but who constitute less than the full part of that population over 65. The police meet them as victims of predatory youth, of burglars, in disputes between neighbors, and as victims of accidents and the disabilities of age.

In terms of public policy the police-relevant problems of the elderly appear amenable to three different basic approaches: (1) improvement of those protections that do not directly involve the police; (2) basic changes in police practices that, although not aimed specifically at the needs of the elderly, benefit them along with other citizens; and (3) basic changes in police practices aimed only or primarily towards the needs of the elderly.

Improvement of protection includes such possibilities as (1) segregating the elderly either in their own high rises or neighborhood areas and thus reducing their risk to young criminals; (2) developing means to make premises more secure against burglary; (3) providing individuals with means to call for assistance while on the street; (4) providing special transportation services for the elderly so as to reduce their vulnerability to street attack; (5) organizing neighborhoods so that residents watch out for each other and develop their own strong norms of conformity and social control that can be enforced most of the time short of police involvement.

This broad range of preventive measures either does not involve the police, or involves them only indirectly. Those measures that involve new building design and technology are already being extensively developed by LEAA. For example, a tiny wrist watch alarm device that broadcasts to the nearest police station and permits instant knowledge of the street location of the victim is being tested. Many of these preventive or protective developments will be useful to all citizens, not just the elderly.

Although technological innovations may inconvenience the criminal and somewhat reduce victimization, the most fundamental source of crime is lack of community development and social control exercised by neighborhood residents over and on behalf of themselves. Neighborhood development in the desperately poor and forgotten neighborhoods of our cities is perhaps the most fundamental domestic problem of our time. The existence of the police, as opposed to a police state, assumes that such development exists, and that the police presence will only be needed in those exceptional instances when community controls break down. To depend upon the police instead of community self-control is to invite disaster.

It may be objected that such control is beyond the capacity of the urban poor, but I think this is patently false. First, it underestimates the capacity and the need of people to create a community in which they can take pride as well as feel safe. Second, there are many examples both in American history and around the world of the poor, even in societies where the contrast of inequality is starker than in our own, developing strong community organization and self-control.

There are two basic changes I would propose to be made in police practices that would benefit not only the elderly but all citizens:

1. At the present time most departments allocate a very large proportion of their resources to patrol; yet we know that a very large proportion of patrol time accomplishes little.[8] According to Reiss as well as others only a tiny percent of patrol time is actually spent on criminal matters.[9] Furthermore, even in this regard, much actual activity is essentially bureaucratic, the making of official records and reports, often to fulfill insurance requirements. Also, the police are often inadequately trained in conflict mediation, and in a knowledge of those public agencies to which the elderly among others might be referred for assistance with their problems, assistance of a more long-term nature. There should be a new division of labor in which bureaucratic activities are carried out

by someone other than a uniformed patrolman. Uniformed patrolmen should not ride randomly within an area as they do now. Rather they should be assigned to stations like firemen and those so assigned should cover only emergencies related to a crime or the maintenance of public or private order or service. Those assigned to this duty should be specialists who should continue to perform such duties through promotion instead of, as now, being promoted out of street work to plain clothes work. Emergency street work should be held in the highest esteem rather than being assigned, as is often the case, to the youngest and least experienced, or least able officers.

2. Police now have a significant portion of their time and attention devoted to control of vices such as gambling, drug addiction, and prostitution.[10] Although these should not be decontrolled, perhaps they might be decriminalized, and alternate forms of control used. These two changes would release a tremendous amount of time of officers, and permit them to become more professional in their pursuit of criminals, and release manpower for emergency street work. In fact, since deterrence is probably more a function of the probability of being caught, than of the severity of punishment, the entire strategy should be to release manpower now wasted on random patrol, taking reports and making ritual busts of local bookies for more serious problems, problems essentially related to increasing the probability that those who commit serious crimes will be caught in the act, or soon thereafter, and promptly punished, or else so the quality of noncriminal service can be improved.

Finally, insofar as special projects aimed only at the elderly are concerned, and exclusively the role of police, the most needed are not so much related directly to crime as to either the results of crime or to the knowledge police gain through the service or other contacts they make. Police have greater opportunity than any other agency to learn of situations of serious need or emergency among elderly citizens. Project Assist was based on such knowledge.[11] It would seem that routine referral should be institutionalized into police procedures, in fact, mandated for the police officer. The effective short-term work of police might then be supplemented by the long-term work of other agencies. Police routinely refer medical emergencies to physicians, and sometimes now, alcohol emergencies to detoxification centers. Since so many of the elderly seek service not related to crime from police or need special services as a result of crime, one of the most useful functions they might provide for the elderly is as a referral agency for this wide variety of problems. Such a function is only possible if police receive more training than many now do, especially in regard to greater sensitivity to the more traumatic effects of victimization of the elderly, and the availability of community resources for long-term assistance. It will also require the social welfare system itself to make itself more accessible to civilians suffering emergencies, since change in police practice cannot occur in isolation.

There are no easy solutions to crime against the elderly or any other large segment of the population. Certainly routine police practice will not solve the problem. Indirect prevention, new means of protection, and emphasis on community development are more likely to be successful than simply more manpower. Those basic changes in the police role and police practice that will benefit the general public will also benefit the elderly. At the present time these seem to be the most promising avenues of approach.

Notes

1. D. Moberg, "Old Age and Crime," *Journal of Criminal Law, Criminology and Police Science*, 43 (March-April, 1953), pp. 764-776.

2. See C. Cunningham, "Crime and the Aging Victim," *Midwest Research Institute Quarterly* (Spring, 1973), pp. 4-9; P.M. Brostoff, R.B. Brown, and R.N. Butler, "The Public Interest: Report No. 6, 'Beating Up' on the Elderly: Police, Social Work, Crime," *Aging and Human Development*, 3 (November, 1972), pp. 319-322; J. Goldsmith and N. Thomas, "Crimes Against the Elderly: A Continuing National Crisis," *Aging*, 237 (July, 1974), pp. 10-13; Law Enforcement Assistance Administration, *Criminal Victimization in the United States* (Washington, D.C.: U.S. Government Printing Office, 1973); Law Enforcement Assistance Administration, *Crime in Eight American Cities* (Washington, D.C.: U.S. Government Printing Office, 1974); and J. Gubrium, "Victimization in Old Age: Available Evidence and Three Hypotheses," *Crime and Delinquency*, 20 (July, 1974), pp. 245-250.

3. A. Reiss, *The Police and the Public* (New Haven: Yale University Press, 1971), pp. 65-70. See also D. Black, "Production of Crime Rates," *American Sociological Review*, 35 (August, 1970), pp. 733-748.

4. Brostoff, Brown, and Butler, "The Public Interest," p. 320.

5. D. Cruse and J. Rubin, "Police Behavior," *Journal of Psychiatry and Law*, 1 (Summer, 1973), pp. 167-222.

6. Reiss, *The Police and the Public*, p. 11, and J. Clark and R. Sykes, "Some Determinants of Police Organization and Practice In a Modern Industrial Democracy," in D. Glaser, ed., *Handbook of Criminology* (Chicago: Rand McNally, 1974), p. 485.

7. A. Stinchcombe, "Institutions of Privacy in the Determination of Police Administrative Practice," *American Journal of Sociology*, 69 (September 1963), pp. 150-160.

8. G. Kelling et al., *The Kansas City Preventive Patrol Experiment: A Technical Report* (Washington, D.C.: Police Foundation, 1974), pp. 533-535.

9. Reiss, *The Police and the Public*, p. 94 ff.

10. J. Rubinstein, *City Police* (New York: Farrar, Straus and Giroux, 1973); J. Skolnick, *Justice Without Trial* (New York: Wiley, 1966).

11. Brostoff, Brown, and Butler, "The Public Interest."

14

The Police Connection: A New Way to Get Information and Referral Services to the Elderly

Phyllis Mensh Brostoff

Crime against the elderly has recently become a much discussed issue.[1] Security is a topic foremost in the minds of many elderly people. A recent survey of needs done by the Milwaukee County Commission on Aging found that "Seventy percent of the sample ranked personal safety as their first, second, or third greatest concern."[2] The fact that many older people in severe need come to the attention of the police when no crime has been committed, however, is not discussed as often.

The Final Report of the White House Conference on Aging included in its recommendations that "social services should be designated to work closely with police departments so that all elderly persons who are victims of crime, or who report noncriminal problems to the police, can obtain all necessary assistance."[3] A prototype of such a social services delivery system, called Project Assist, was demonstrated in Washington, D.C. from October 1970 through April 1971.[a] The following is a description of Project Assist and a consideration of how the ideas for developing a linkage with the police as a source for both finding the isolated elderly, and helping elderly victims of crime, demonstrated by Project Assist could become a regular part of the Information and Referral Services mandated under Title III of the Older Americans Act.

Project Assist

In June 1970, the Office of Services to the Aged, Washington, D.C. government, awarded a contract to the Washington School of Psychiatry to study the relationship between older people and the Metropolitan Police Department. The purposes of the research contract were:

1. To determine the extent to which older persons are victims of crime in the District of Columbia.

The author gratefully acknowledges the pioneering thought and efforts of Roberta B. Brown and Robert N. Butler, M.D., in identifying how the elderly come to the attention of the police, and in developing Project Assist to demonstrate the important link the police can be between the isolated elderly and the services they need.

[a]For the full report on Project Assist see "Metropolitan Police Contacts with the Elderly," Appendix II of the District of Columbia Report to the 1971 White House Conference on Aging; Washington, D.C.: Washington School of Psychiatry, 1971. A limited number of copies are available from the author: Phyllis Mensh Brostoff, 3000 North Stowell Avenue, Milwaukee, Wisconsin 53211.

2. To discover what social or health problems result from such victimization and how they are dealt with.
3. To ascertain under what circumstances older persons come to the attention of the police when no crime has been committed, but aid of police is sought because other community resources are unknown or not available.
4. To explore methods and techniques for quick and appropriate referral for service by police in disposing of problems of older persons encountered as victims of crime or as persons needing or seeking help.[4]

The research project began on September 1, 1970.[b] It was decided to attack purpose no. 4 first; that is, to immediately begin working out a practical means of getting appropriate social services to many old people who came into contact with the police. Since a number of technical difficulties in beginning the overall survey of types of contacts with the police were encountered, especially since no such study had ever been done before, it was felt that actual experience would provide data as well as a basis for citywide survey later in the project year. The demonstration social service referral system was designated Project Assist, a name designed to suggest help to both old people and the police.

It was hoped, then, that Project Assist could demonstrate the utility of social service personnel to the Police Department at the same time that it could find out the dimensions of victimization of old people and the use by the aged of the police as a "social service" agency. The outcome would be a model for social service agencies to use the police as a case-finding resource and also provide specific knowledge about the extent and type of victimization of the aged in Washington, D.C.

The Police and Social Problems

Any program that seeks to work with a big city police department must reflect an understanding of the pressures and controversies that surround the role of the police in our society.

The police are the only agency that is both constantly present and always visible on the street. The use of paramilitary uniforms and the carrying of guns and other visible signs of authority serve to reinforce both the public and the police view of the police as an agency of social control. However, in reality a large percentage of police time is actually spent on noncriminal matters.[c]

---

[b]The service giving part of the project was in full swing from mid-October 1970, through mid-April 1971, with some continuation through June. Further data were collected and all data were analyzed from mid-April through June. The final report was written in July and August 1971.

[c]A number of authorities who suggest changing the role definition of the police to conform more to the reality of the high percentage of police time spent on noncriminal matters mention the need for redesigning police uniforms to look less militaristic. For example, see: Vaupel, Carl F., Jr., "Improving Police Effectiveness and Police Relations," *Police*, Vol. 15, September-October 1970, pp. 19-20.

Therefore, the modern police officer faces a complex problem of role definition. He is a public servant, but he is also an enforcer of laws. He does help individuals, but his main focus is on the criminal, not the victim. The problems of our society are complex in the extreme but most often the police officer is a "nonprofessional," a high-school graduate without extensive training in dealing with the human problems he is confronted with daily. But professionalization, if this means sending police officers to college, would not solve the problem of conflict between the roles of the helper versus the enforcer. It would not help the officer in performing the standard, daily duty of "preventive patrol," which often means walking or riding around a beat on which nothing of significance happens.

A major thrust in police planning in the last decade has been the development of "police-community relations" officers, programs, committees, jobs, pamphlets, and a host of other methods. "Police-community relations" has been seized upon as a panacea to solve a great number of community and police problems including the need for job programs for youths, the need to control potential riot situations, the need to improve the image of the police department, the need to represent the police department at community meetings, forums, and so forth, plus a variety of educative functions such as teaching citizens how to prevent burglaries, a central emergency telephone number to call, and school safety programs. Frequently, the real meaning of "police-community relations" is to improve relations between the police department and the minority, particularly the black, inner-city community.[5] Clearly, the list of types of programs developed under the rubric of "police-community relations" is almost unending.

But what are the police, after all, if not a community service? Can a special unit effectively "handle" police-community relations when most officers have contact with the public daily? Can crime be substantially reduced in a free society without the alleviation of the socioeconomic problems that cause it? Since youth commit by far the largest number of crimes, can crime be controlled without programs oriented toward youth? Since people come to the police when they are in a crisis situation even when that crisis is not related to a crime, how can a police department expect to perform its function without working in cooperation with other community service agencies?

It is obvious that a reordering of the method of delivering the services the community offers its citizens is needed. Many different programs have been suggested or attempted that do provide at least part of the solution to the problem of what to do about linking up the police department with the rest of the city's services so as to direct individuals who have social problems to the agencies set up to help them. However, several elements are consistently missing from the literature on "police-community" relations. One of these elements is a concern for the victims of crime. Little is ever said of following up cases of criminal victimization with an offer of social service help. Another missing element is any questioning of the ability of a 17- or 18-year-old indigenous, nonprofessional to help people who are the victims of crime or who are suffering from the consequences of other social problems. The real purpose of these programs is to employ young people and they are based on the unquestioned assumption that these individuals can do a thoroughly adequate job. These programs suggest that all that is necessary for getting help to clients is a traffic director who can motion the individual, sheeplike, to the proper social agency enclosure. In reality, social service information and referral is a far more complex process.

A third element is the absence of criticism of social service agencies for not making the effort themselves to use the police as a primary case-finding resource. It is, after all, the business of social agencies to work on the solution of the social problems of the community; yet the police are apparently expected to encompass the tasks of social control and the provision of social services to the population.

It is possible, in fact, that the relatively poor state of police-community relations is directly related to the poor outreach and lack of significant social change that has been promulgated by other community agencies in most cities. One might ask whether the police departments might actually be taking a "bum rap" for the failure of these other agencies.

How Project Assist Functioned

At the suggestion of the Police Department, it was decided that Project Assist would operate in the Third Police District. The Third District was geographically the smallest police district in Washington. It was an area with a dense population, a relatively large mixture of whites and blacks, and three high-rise public housing buildings for the elderly within its boundaries and two just beyond them. Thus, it was believed that a substantial number of people over 60 resided in the area. It was also the area that had the highest crime rate in the District of Columbia. By late October 1970, an office was opened in the first floor of a small house opposite the Third District headquarters.

Project Assist felt that the house was a highly acceptable alternative to an office in the stationhouse because of the high noise level and great overcrowding in the stationhouse. This meant, however, that continuous informal interaction with individual police officers was limited. Client contact, however, was facilitated and clients walking into the stationhouse were encouraged to go across the street when it was appropriate.

The first few cases Project Assist handled concerned individuals (people 60 or over) who walked into the police station requesting help. These cases averaged about three or four a week. Project Assist also found cases by examining police records. In this connection the inspector of the Third District gave permission for the director of Project Assist to read the police forms recording crimes and incidents that concerned complainants age 60 or over. After a period of uncertainty, a regular system was worked out where a desk officer would pull the reports on Tuesdays and Fridays. This meant the reports were about events that happened one to three or four days earlier.

The criteria by which reports were selected for follow-up by Project Assist were:

1. *Type of crime:* If the crime was one in which the individual was present, such as robbery or assault, or if the material stolen suggested a need existed that might be vital and difficult to fill, such as an income check or food stamps, the case was chosen.
2. *Type of incident:* If the incident was a fall or a death of a close relative (spouse, sibling, etc.), the need for an ambulance, a report of a missing person or something of this nature, suggesting an underlying social problem, the case was selected.
3. *Employment of the individual:* If the person was reported as "unemployed" or "retired" the case was selected. People who appeared to be regular members of the work force were excluded.

The reasoning behind these criteria was simple: Of the 60 or so cases reported in the Third District each week involving people 60 or over, which cases suggested the existence of social problems? A person who has been present at his criminal victimization, or has had to call the police to go to the hospital, or has lost a wife or husband, and who also appears not to have any regular contact with society every day through work, might either have a social problem or find it very difficult to handle the consequences of being criminally victimized. It is important to realize that very often police officers categorize 80- or 90-year-old people as being unemployed, when in fact they are unemployable and have been out of the work force for years. It was Project Assist's observation that the only people categorized as "retired" in police reports were people who were moderately well off. Their response to a police officer's question about their work status was that they were retired; they, in fact, had a retirement. But other people, too poor throughout their lives to have had much, if any, pension, appeared to have worked until they could no longer get jobs and did not see themselves as retired but rather unemployed. These were people generally in the poorest circumstances and most in need of aggressive case finding in order to connect them with the social service system.

Aside from people who walked in, or who were found through police records, a third method of case finding was used. That was one in which other people contacted Project Assist requesting that help be rendered to a person known to them. Police officers were the largest source of this type of contact, and this method proved to be one of the most important elements in working with the police in finding the isolated elderly. For example, one police officer had noticed two old women in a first-floor room every time he went into a row house to which he was called every month or so to investigate various disturbances. The two old women were living in one room, without a refrigerator or stove. They both were very eccentric and poor, and apparently there were several men who lived in the house and bought alcohol with the women's very small social security checks. This kind of complex social problem was often seen by officers but rarely connected by them with a social agency. Other social agencies also began requesting help from Project Assist. Because these agencies did not make home visits, many of them were quick to use a service that did make such visits.

The individuals whose cases were pulled from police records were contacted in a number of ways. The first attempt was by telephone: if the person had a phone, he was called and the project was briefly described. An offer of help was then made, specifying various kinds of areas in which help might be needed, including increasing income, food stamps, information about agencies, and the like. A good number of individuals were found who were eligible for public assistance yet were unaware of the existence of these benefits. Information was often requested about applying for public housing, getting food stamps, Medicaid, and so forth. Often an appointment was set up for the social worker to visit the person in the home, or to have an appropriate form or other service (such as an application for public assistance or Medicaid, or a public health nurse) sent out to the person's home, or to help fill out one of these forms after it had arrived.

If the person could not be reached at home by telephone, a home visit was attempted. However, since buildings were often locked or the person was not at home, this was not as successful as a third method, which was to send a letter with an explanation of the project and an offer of help. Although a great many of the clients were illiterate, they often had ways to have mail read to them and also they could read numbers. Therefore, many clients called the office once they had the telephone number. Probably, a number of the letters that were never responded to or were returned by the Post Office were sent to the people who did not have a phone and who also did not have a system to have their mail read. These may well represent the hardest to reach and most needy elderly.

Positive need was uncovered in this way (through police records), but another problem was found, that of dealing with the fear resulting from having been criminally victimized. Project Assist did help the tenant council in one public housing high-rise request the new ultra-bright street lights installed in the area around the building. Aside from this, little else positive could be offered to comfort people suffering mainly from fear. However, a number of clients did express relief at the chance to talk about their victimization and from learning that the police department was involved in a continuing interest in them. For many, contact through a public agency such as the police was unexpected, and a comfort. In effect, it humanized the police department for these individuals.

Several dramatic examples of how valuable a resource the police are for helping the most needy elderly are the following:

Mrs. R

An officer left a note for the Project Assist social worker, asking her to investigate the situation of Mrs. R., no other information was offered.

Unable to get anything but a busy signal from Mrs. R.'s telephone, the social worker went to Mrs. R.'s address. The door to the apartment was ajar in the moderate-income building in which she lived, certainly an unusual circumstance. Since no one answered, the social worker walked in. The apartment was small, very crowded, but moderately clean. A terribly thin woman was lying on top of the bed, sleeping deeply. Unable to rouse the woman, who the social worker assumed was Mrs. R., the worker went to find the resident manager for information. He said that Mrs. R. had been sick, and that he and a friend of hers had tried to get her to go to the hospital Saturday night. They had called the police for an ambulance, but when it arrived, Mrs. R. refused to go. This was how the police officer met Mrs. R. The resident manager said he had contacted her son in Florida and that he expected the son to arrive any time. Since it appeared that the situation was in hand with the imminent arrival of the son, the social worker left, leaving her name and phone number with the manager to give to the son if help was needed. The next day, having heard nothing from the son or the manager, and still unable to get Mrs. R. on the phone, the worker went back and saw that Mrs. R. was in even worse shape. Semiconscious, Mrs. R. was unable to respond to simple questions; she appeared to be dying from malnutrition and dehydration. An ambulance was summoned and she was taken to the closest hospital to her home, since at this time she could not refuse hospitalization. The manager had given the worker the name of the man he understood to be Mrs. R.'s doctor. The social worker called him to have him contact the hospital and arrange for Mrs. R.'s admission, but since it was after 5:00 P.M. the doctor could not be reached. The worker was worried that the private hospital would think Mrs. R. had no insurance and would send her in her very severe condition across town to D.C. General Hospital. But since she had no more information about Mrs. R., this was the best the worker could do. The next morning the social worker found out that indeed the hospital had sent her to D.C. General. The doctors at D.C. General felt that Mrs. R. was dying and it was almost a hopeless case, a situation that should have kept Mrs. R. at the private hospital if it had followed established guidelines to transfer noninsured patients only when they were not emergencies. However, Mrs. R. did live, thanks to the expert care she received at D.C. General. Her son arrived several days later. If the police officer had not called in Project Assist, Mrs. R. would almost certainly have died in her room all alone before her son ever reached Washington.

Mr. D.

Mr. D. came into Project Assist's office because his wife was missing. He had been in the hospital with pneumonia and she had visited him the day before his release. When he returned home she was gone, but she had not packed her clothes or anything else. She had taken only her pocketbook, which contained their food stamps and public assistance money for the month. Mr. D. had no use of his right hand or arm from a 40-year-old injury and was unable to "even open a can of beans," as he put it. A neighbor had been helping him keep his place clean and preparing some food. The social worker, by having the need certified by a public health nurse, was able to arrange with public assistance to add money to Mr. D.'s check so the neighbor could be paid and thus continue this needed help with housekeeping. Over the next month and a half Mr. D. stopped by Project Assist a number of times to gain some reassurance that the police had not found his wife (checks with the morgue and hospitals, etc., all proved futile), and to have the social worker explain how to use the extra money from public assistance. A month and a half after the first contact, Mr. D. came into the office with a letter from D.C. General Hospital, asking him if he knew a woman who fit his wife's description but who had a slightly different name. Mr. D., was overcome with anticipation. He did not have a telephone, so the social worker called the hospital social worker and established that, in fact, this was Mrs. D. She had been brought into the hospital by police officers from another district on the day after Mr. D. had left the hospital. Mrs. D. had neither identification, coat, nor shoes, and was suffering from extreme cold (this was January). She perhaps had been robbed and knocked down and lost her memory as a result. The hospital was keeping her as a social emergency, although she no longer needed hospital care, because they could not find out anything about her until she finally remembered she had visited Mr. D. in the hospital the month before. She had not even remembered he was her husband. Project Assist arranged to have the extra housekeeping money continued until Mrs. D. had made a full recovery of her memory and faculties at home.

Mrs. Y

Mrs. Y., aged 65, black and a widow, lived alone and had just retired from a federal job. A hard worker, she had never taken leave in years and thus was living on extended leave until she used up her time before formally retiring. Mrs. Y.'s pocketbook was snatched in the hallway of her building and Project Assist called to offer help if this presented her with any problems. Since she had sufficient money, she was able to sustain the loss of her purse, but she did need help in arranging for an application to a public housing project. Project Assist helped her with this, over a period of approximately two weeks, using the telephone only. At ten o'clock one morning Mrs. Y. called Project Assist and reported she had been approached a few days before by two men who said they were police officers. They had shown her some photographs and she identified the person who had taken her pocketbook. Then these men told her that in order to catch the thief she would have to give them $5,000 (all of her savings). She agreed, but the cautious bank teller had refused to give her the entire amount in cash, insisting on giving her mostly cashier's checks. Mrs. Y. was to meet the men in half an hour to go with them to cash these checks. She said she was beginning to question the situation and decided to call Project Assist. Project Assist immediately alerted a sergeant in the stationhouse across the street, and he called Mrs. Y., got a description of what she would be wearing, and sent several men to the meeting place (luckily only a few blocks away). The two men were apprehended when they pulled their car into a gas station. Almost all of Mrs. Y.'s money was recovered in what the Inspector said was the largest amount of money recovered in a robbery in the Third District.

Characteristics of the Clients Serviced
by Project Assist[d]

Project Assist had contact with 220 clients in its seven months of direct services. These 220 clients were a selection from all of the older people who came into contact with the Third District police in this period. They do not represent a sample, since they were either picked in a purposeful manner or were individuals who walked into the police station or who were put in contact with Project Assist by friends or police officers. The analysis, therefore, is suggestive of what this particular kind of project encounters, but is not an unbiased sample of the over-60 population that could potentially have contact with the police. The information presented is given for the purpose of a beginning evaluation of how effective a program of this type can be, and to point the way in an exploratory manner to an understanding of the relationship between the elderly, the police, and community services.

The mean age of Project Assist's clients (where age was known) was 70 years. Robbery was the most common criminal problem. The most common noncrime-related problem was physical illness. This was expected because this was one of the criteria for picking a case from the records. Forty-two (19 percent) of the cases began with multiple social problems. Many more actually did have multiple problems, of course.

Looking at sex and race, 63 percent of the clients were female and 36 percent were male. This is a higher proportion of females than in the population of the city as a whole. Just over 50 percent of the cases concerned black people, and in 16 percent of the cases the race of the individual was unknown. Only a little less than a third of the cases where race was known concerned white people. Forty percent of the clients were classified as severely impaired and only 13 percent were not impaired at all. This description of the client's impairment was a judgment of the social worker (project director). Thirteen percent of the cases received their income from Public Assistance. This is substantially more than the 6 percent of old people citywide who were receiving public assistance at that time. Almost 20 percent of the people received income from social security plus other sources. Twelve percent of the people had social security as their sole source of income, and 5 percent of the people had no source of income at all.

The largest group of people where family status was known was that of widows and widowers (30 percent) and 15 percent were single. Thirty-five percent of these people had lived in Washington a long time. Sixty-five percent of the people had a telephone and one third did not. More than half of the

[d]For further statistical analysis of crime against the elderly as reported in police records in Washington, D.C., in Fiscal Year 1970 see Chapters X and XI of "Metropolitan Police Contacts with the Elderly."

clients of Project Assist were people who, according to police records, had contacted the police themselves and who Project Assist then identified from the police file. Twenty-five percent of the people either walked in themselves or a friend or neighbor walked in or called Project Assist or the police. Two-thirds of the clients were in contact with Project Assist for only a few days. Project Assist was unable to contact 21 percent of the individuals whom it attempted to help.

As far as could be determined, nearly all of the people on whom Project Assist had information were known to at least one social agency, with only 4.5 percent not known to any agency. Of course, many of the agencies (for example, Social Security) did not really offer any social services. After the first month or so of service, Project Assist began sending a letter offering help to clients without phones whom it found hard to reach. These individuals represented about 27 percent of the clients Project Assist had. Of these, 57 percent did not reply to the letter, and 43 percent did reply.

Looking at the disposition of the cases, no contact was made in about 21 percent of the cases. No help was needed in 13 percent and no help was able to be given in about 2 percent of the cases. Some help was given in 31 percent of the cases. These categories were designated by the social worker and director.

By the phrase "help was given," it is meant that some relief for the presenting and/or underlying problem was available, offered, and accepted. This does not imply that the person was permanently helped or even that the helping agency was in long-term contact with the individual. But at least some relief for the individual's problems was extended.

Information and Referral Services

Although Project Assist was limited in its scope, it seems to be highly suggestive of a valuable expansion of information and referral services.

Recently a great multiplication of information and referral services has taken place in many American communities.[6] Briefly defined, the functions of information and referral services are (1) to link people in need with the appropriate agency or service designed to eliminate or alleviate that need, and (2) to assist the long-range community planning processes by discovering gaps, overlaps, and duplications in services.[7] The most recent theoretical work done on information and referral services encourages the development of a coordinated network of fairly autonomous information and referral centers, each of which would deliver one or more discrete modules of functions designed to facilitate access to human services. These modules include information, referral, systematic follow-up, escort, and outreach.[8] It is generally recognized that "the effectiveness of programs that serve low-income persons or those with social needs depends on the staff available to do outreach or follow-up."[9] The National Standards for Information and Referral state that "The Service shall continually seek to maximize channels of access to needed services for all persons included in the area of service."[10] Finally, the Federal Regulations for the Older Americans Act Title III Comprehensive Service Amendments of 1973 state that the Area Agencies on Aging "take steps designed to achieve the establishment or maintenance of information and referral sources in sufficient numbers so that all older persons will have reasonably convenient access to such sources by the end of fiscal year 1975."[11]

As far as the author can tell, aside from Project Assist, no other attempt has been made to link elderly victims of crime, or older people who come to the police for help when no crime has been committed, with services that might help them with the social problems they bring to the police.[e] Yet, the author believes that an important way to maximize access to services for a particularly needy subgroup of the elderly, could be established by the outreach component of local information and referral services using the police as a source for finding clients and making the information and referral services available to the police as a resource for handling problems the police are not equipped to handle.

This could be accomplished in two ways. The first would be to inform all police officers, with special emphasis on patrolmen and their sergeants, of the existence of the central information and referral service. This would hopefully be a single telephone number as presently exists in Milwaukee.[f] Small, wallet-sized cards could be printed, which would be distributed to all duty officers. An outreach worker could systematically attend training sessions and the daily "roll calls," which most police systems use to inform each new shift of information needed for the day's patrol, explain the service, hand out the information cards, and answer questions. Officers would be encouraged to both call the number themselves with referrals for service and tell people they encounter in their daily work who might need social services about the existence of the information service.

The second major device would be the use of police records to follow up on elderly victims of crime. The author believes this would not unreasonably impinge upon the confidentiality of the records if it is done on a "limited access" basis where "information is released to persons for use in specifically designated purposes for which a compelling public interest can be shown."[12] However, it would obviously require a willing and cooperative police department, such as the one in Washington, D.C., during the duration of Project Assist.

Each community would probably want to consider different criteria in developing outreach through the follow-up of police records. For example, if

[e]Neither the survey by Goldsmith and Tomas mentioned above or a survey by Erich M. Franz called *The Elderly as Victims of Crime*, Milwaukee Urban Observatory, University of Wisconsin-Milwaukee, January 1975 (Mimeographed), mention any other project of this sort.

[f]For further information about the Milwaukee information and referral system write to Wisconsin Information Service-Milwaukee, 161 W. Wisconsin Avenue, Milwaukee, Wisconsin.

resources for outreach are limited, as they are likely to be, perhaps only records in the police precincts in areas known to have a concentration of the elderly poor would be canvassed. Criteria such as the ones used by Project Assist for deciding which cases to follow up, might be used to specify further the most needy target group. Further research into the kind and effect of a criminal victimization of the elderly would no doubt suggest other criteria to be used. The outreach workers should probably be required to make repeated home visits in order to contact individuals without telephones who did not respond to letters because these are perhaps the most isolated and needy elderly in the community.

Perhaps a final word might be useful on the special knowledge that work on Project Assist gave to the author about the functioning of one metropolitan police department. Except for workers in probation and parole departments, very few social workers have professional contacts with the police department. It is, however, useful to understand the hierarchical organizational system of the police department in order to be effective in working with it.[g] Furthermore, the tone of a department and a precinct house is set by the officers. If the outreach effort has the approval and is promoted by the officers, the man on the beat will act accordingly. All patrolmen and uniformed officers wear (again this is in Washington, D.C.) name tags. This is very helpful to an outreach worker in establishing a good relationship with individuals who can then become a source for identifying needy elderly whom they see in their daily patrol but who have not been victimized by a specific crime. Finally, outreach workers should also be prepared for the noise and apparent confusion of a station house.[h]

Conclusion

In summary, the police represent a potent source for finding the isolated elderly. The role of the police in our society is a complex and difficult one and other community agencies must be willing to accept their responsibility for the development of expanded services rather than assume the police alone can handle all cases of social need that come to them. Rather than the development of a new social service agency, the Information and Referral services mandated

---

[g]Clothing is one useful key to the organizational structure. The lowest ranking individuals, the workers (patrolmen) wear blue shirts. The highest ranking patrolmen are sergeants who wear stripes on their blue shirts. The officers (starting with lieutenant) all wear white shirts. The detectives (a much coveted position of patrolman-rank individuals) wear business suits. Finally (at least in Washington, D.C., during the duration of Project Assist), the "mod squad" or undercover agents (usually narcotics) wear old or "mod" clothes.

[h]Many of these buildings are old and obsolescent in the amount of space they offer, so many functions take place in virtually the same area (police officers filing reports, people asking for information, officers booking suspects, stolen loot being catalogued, calls being relayed to patrol cars, etc.).

under the Comprehensive Service Amendments of 1973 of the Older Americans Act should step in and fill the gap that exists for services to both elderly victims of crime and other needy people with severe social problems who come to the attention of the police.

Notes

1. See Goldsmith, Jack, and Tomas, Noel E., "Crimes Against the Elderly: A Continuing National Crisis," *Aging*, June-July 1974.

2. Mayrl, Robin Bieger, and Witzel, Verna Lee, *Program Needs of Milwaukee County's Older Adults*, Milwaukee County Commission on Aging, April 1975 (Mimeographed), p. 51.

3. *Toward a National Policy on Aging*, Final Report of the White House Conference on Aging, Volume II; Washington, D.C.: 1973, p. 235.

4. Social Services Administration, Human Resources Department, Washington, D.C. Government, Contract No. 70582, August 12, 1970, pp. 1-2.

5. President's Commission on Law Enforcement and Administration of Justice, *The Challenge of Crime in a Free Society*, Washington, D.C.: U.S. Government Printing Office, 1967, p. 99.

6. Long, Nicholas, "Information and Referral Services: A Short History and Some Recommendations," *Social Service Review*, Volume 47, No. 1, March 1973, p. 49.

7. United Way of America, *National Standards: Information and Referral Services*, Arlington, Virginia, February 1973, p. 1.

8. Long, "Information and Referral Services," p. 53.

9. Lovell, Beverly, "Information and Referral Service: Insights and Affirmations," *Public Welfare*, Volume 33, No. 1, Winter 1975, p. 41.

10. United Way of America, *National Standards*, p. 9.

11. Federal Register, Volume 38, No. 196, Thursday, October 11, 1973, p. 28039.

12. Stallings, C.W., "Local Information Policy: Confidentiality and Public Access," *Public Administration Review*, Volume 34, No. 3, May-June 1974, p. 201.

15 Public Housing Security and the Elderly: Practice versus Theory

David P. Van Buren

For the purpose of analyzing security policy, it may be useful to conceptualize the public housing project as a sociotechnical system, an organic unit characterized by the interaction of its social and physical environments. In such a system, one might reasonably expect deterioration in one environment to bring about deterioration in the other. W. Ross Ashby, for example, in his model of self-regulation and requisite variety, tells us that, for an organic system to survive, it must be able not only to maintain and regulate itself internally but also to adapt to its external environment.[a] What does all of this have to do with public housing security and the elderly? It is the thesis here that elements of our traditional approach to security have not prevented and, indeed, may have contributed to our perception of public housing projects as "fearful environments."

As Professor Sherman (Chapter 6) has already pointed out, our study examined the incidence and fears of criminal victimization among the elderly in three different types of public housing projects. When respondents were asked how safe they felt in their buildings, there was a marked difference between those living in age-segregated buildings and those in age-integrated sites. In both the age-segregated and mixed projects, 2 percent of the elderly tenants said they were fearful of being in their buildings during the day whereas approximately 15 percent expressed having similar fears at night. In the totally age-integrated project, however, 31 percent of the respondents were fearful during the day, and 72 percent were afraid of being criminally victimized at night. Since merely asking people how safe they feel at different places and at different times may not provide an accurate indication of the impact of such fears, a more rigorous indicator of dissatisfaction was employed. When asked if they felt there was so much crime in their project that they wished they could move, no respondents residing in the age-segregated and mixed settings expressed a desire to move. In contrast, 42 percent of the elderly tenants in age-integrated buildings wished to move. Many, in fact, had already made arrangements to do so at the time of our

---

This chapter deals with the second facet of the study outlined by Edmund A. Sherman, Evelyn S. Newman, and Anne D. Nelson in Chapter 6. It reviews the security practices of the three public housing sites previously discussed, and examines the relationship between elderly residents' fears of crime and the practice of security in their respective projects.

[a]Ashby presents a more detailed discussion of regulation and requisite variety in biological systems in Chapters 10 and 11 of his work: W. Ross Ashby, *An Introduction to Cybernetics* (London: Chapman & Hall, Ltd., 1961), p. 212.

interviews. In light of this, the question before us is two-fold. In what way are the social environments of the three projects related to their respective security practices, and what impact do formal security organizations have upon residents' fears?

Traditionally, many security organizations serving public housing have employed what might be termed "the armed fortress" approach. Guards and locks are often viewed as the prime mechanisms of crime prevention, and the need for more guards and better locks seems ceaselessly to follow a perceived lack of security. Patrol is the game, and deterrence is often its name. Just as there are financial costs to such an approach, there are social costs. If security is viewed as a balance between freedom and control, then locks and guards may offer certain unanticipated consequences. To the extent that it effectively prevents undesirable outsiders from entering buildings and apartments, "the armed fortress" approach may simultaneously discourage insiders from venturing out. At best, however, this is mere speculation. The more serious consequence of such an approach appears to be the deterrent effect it often has on the willingness of residents to participate, even minimally, in bearing the burden of their mutual security. Fortunately, a new model for security and crime prevention in public housing has evolved in recent years—Oscar Newman's concept of "defensible space."

In what is rapidly becoming a classic in its field, Newman's approach integrates elements of mechanical prevention with an architectural model of corrective prevention.[1] As he defines it, defensible space uses physical design to attack the attitudes and structure of motivations that allow the criminal event to occur. He states, "*Defensible space* is a model for residential environments which inhibits crime by creating the physical expression of a social fabric that defends itself."[2] By altering the physical environment to create perceived zones of influence under tenant control, by maximizing the capacity and utility of natural surveillance, and by changing the image and milieu of public housing projects, Newman proposes the creation of what we have called a self-regulating, sociotechnical system. His approach is sociotechnical because he uses physical design to create a social environment. It is self-regulating because its objective is to restore those mechanisms of informal social control that have often been attributed, perhaps nostalgically, to a more rural society.

It is interesting to speculate whether Oscar Newman's evolution of the concept of defensible space was consciously guided by any single theory of crime. In his book, for example, he writes, "Ghetto leaders and social scientists have challenged us in our belief that crime, born of a poverty of means, opportunity, education, and representation, could be prevented architecturally."[3] Although he cloaks the argument of ghetto leaders and social scientists within the idiom of what Hirschi has termed "strain theory,"[b] Newman, in his

[b]Generally, "strain theory" refers to the perspective that great pressure is necessary before man, who is perceived as a moral being, will engage in deviant or criminal behavior. Hirschi outlines many of the assumptions underlying strain theories in Chapter 1 of his *Causes of Delinquency*. Travis Hirschi, *Causes of Delinquency* (Berkeley: University of California Press, 1969), pp. 4-10.

155

approach, does not address the "causes" of crime in any conventional sense. His perspective is not so much what "causes" crime as what "prevents" the criminal event from occurring. Thus, there is a shift from a problem, phrased in terms of causal analysis, to a mode of intervention based on policy alternatives.[c] It is the latter, however, and not causal analysis that seems frequently to guide the operations of security.

In the light of Newman's work, it is our contention that age-segregated housing for the elderly is an embodiment of defensible space. Whether located in high-rise or low-rise buildings,[d] age-segregated public housing offers, by design, a social environment in which residents share information about one another. In so doing, they often come to define their territorial boundaries, are able to identify outsiders, and participate in the basic regulation of their own security. In terms of the level of patrol activity and the structural formality of security organizations, three different patterns of security emerged in the projects we studied. The age-integrated project was characterized by the active patrol of a formally organized, paid security staff. On any given evening, between seven and nine guards would actively patrol the buildings and grounds. In the age-segregated building located in the mixed setting, only one member of a formally organized, paid security staff served the building. On duty each evening between 4:00 P.M. and midnight, the guard generally employed a passive style, monitoring the door by sitting at a front desk. The security operations of the totally age-segregated site were at the other extreme. No formal security organization of any type existed there. Tenants informally carried out the passive door-monitoring function.

The evolution of informal social groups with the capacity to perform a natural surveillance function appeared to be one of the great assets of the age-segregated buildings. The development of the ability of tenants to identify each other, to perceive outsiders as such, and to question strangers as to their purpose were primary elements in the informal security structure of both the age-segregated and mixed projects. At no time during the course of our study, for example, were any interviewers questioned as to their purpose while entering the age-integrated buildings. This pattern was a reversal of our experiences at the age-segregated and mixed sites where groups of people often gathered socially in front lobbies.

Our interviews also indicated an apparently higher degree of social isolation

---

[c]James Q. Wilson very perceptively discusses the dangers of confusing causal analysis with policy analysis. Rejecting the causal fallacy that problems cannot be solved unless their causes are removed, he argues, "If we regard any crime-prevention or crime-reduction program as defective because it does not address the 'root causes' of crime, then we shall commit ourselves to futile acts that frustrate the citizen while they ignore the criminal." James Q. Wilson, "Crime and the Criminologists," *Commentary*, LVIII (July, 1974), p. 49.

[d]Professor Lawton's research on housing for the elderly appears to support this point. Although noting that some elderly persons dislike living in high-rise buildings, he notes, "If we assume a project will serve only the elderly, so far as we know there is no clear evidence to favor one or the other type of structure for security purposes." M. Powell Lawton, *Planning and Managing Housing for the Elderly* (New York: John Wiley & Sons, Inc., 1975), p. 141.

and anonymity among elderly residents in the age-integrated setting. When respondents were asked how many persons in their building they knew well enough to visit with, nearly 80 percent of those in the age-integrated buildings said they knew less than four. This is significant when one notes that fully 38 percent said they did not know anyone at all sufficiently well to visit with them. In contrast, over 54 percent of those in the age-segregated building said they knew four or more persons that well. Interestingly, the two projects were extremely similar in terms of the length of time respondents had lived there. Sixty-four percent of those in the age-integrated buildings had lived there for more than three years, as compared with 65 percent in the fully age-segregated project. Thus, differences in length of residence did not account for the marked differences in the number of people residents knew in their buildings. Since the age-segregated building in the mixed project was less than one year old, it has been excluded from our comparison.

It is clear from our analysis that the level of patrol activity and the structural formality of security organization are not in themselves major factors in reducing the fears of victimization of elderly tenants. Although the pattern emerges that residents' fears of crime in their building increase as the level of patrol activity and formality of organization increase, one should be cautious about confusing cause with effect. As the level of criminal activity and fear of victimization increased at the age-integrated site, for example, it appears that the activity and formality of security organization were purposively increased as a reaction to this. The important question, however, is whether public housing security for the elderly will be reactive in approach or proactive by design. More guards and better locks, although important considerations, tend to respond reactively to the problems of crime and fears generated by it. On the other hand, age-segregated public housing seems proactively to anticipate the problem by constructing a social environment that reduces the probability of the criminal event. Not only does it appear to offer a more secure environment for the elderly but it seems simultaneously to reduce some of the social isolation and anonymity often associated with the public housing way of life. This then is the essence of defensible space.

As a final note, it may be useful for us to ask what way criminological research and theory may meaningfully guide security practice. Defensible space certainly provides a fruitful example, but the practical implications of criminological theories have sometimes had unanticipated consequences of a less desirable nature. One theory of crime, for example, postulates that crime is caused by a conflict between aspirations and legitimate opportunities for achieving them. Implicitly, crime can be reduced either by increasing legitimate opportunities or by bringing aspirations down to a level commensurate with existing opportunities. Hirschi's control theory, in contrast, views the latter alternative as weakening those bonds to society that help to prevent criminal behavior.[4] From this, one might infer that raising aspirations might reduce crime. This approach, however, is anathema to strain theory.

Ironically, even the alternative of increasing legitimate opportunities, when put into practice, may not resolve the problem. The well-intentioned objectives of providing better housing opportunities and eliminating the blight of urban slums were factors leading to the construction of some public housing projects. Yet, as Richard Cloward and Lloyd Ohlin point out, it was this very slum clearance and the construction of low-income public housing that helped to destroy the remnants of informal social control that were so critical to the security of the communities that preceded them.[e] As areas of defensible space, age-segregated public housing for the elderly, as we have advocated here, attempts to restore some of these mechanisms of social control. As an approach to residential security, its perspective is not the criminal but rather the frequently neglected, potential victim. As a framework for action, it is not so much aimed at the ultimate, immutable causes of crime as it is directed toward developing a social technology of prevention.

Notes

1. Oscar Newman, *Defensible Space* (New York: Collier Books, 1973), p. 4.

2. Ibid., p. 3.

3. Ibid., p. 11.

4. Travis Hirschi, *Causes of Delinquency* (Berkeley: University of California Press, 1969), p. 171.

[e]Cloward and Ohlin point out, "Most low-income housing programs destroy what vestiges of social organization remain in the slum community, in part because they fail to give priority in reoccupancy to site tenants. As a result, traditional residents are displaced and dispersed to other areas of the city, and persons who are strangers to one another are assembled in the housing project." Richard A. Cloward and Lloyd E. Ohlin, *Delinquency and Opportunity* (Glencoe, Ill.: The Free Press of Glencoe, 1960), p. 209.

16 The California Experience in Crime Prevention Programs with Senior Citizens

Evelle J. Younger

Someone has said a nation is judged by its treatment of its youth and its elderly.

Our senior citizens are a minority group that has not had from government leadership the kind of attention their special problems merit, particularly from the criminal justice system—this in spite of their being a minority we all join if we are lucky. In the 1960s when most other minority groups were marching in protest and turning over police cars to dramatize inequities, the senior citizen minority was not.

However, this minority has experience, understanding, and an increasing willingness to act to improve their situation. This is why the title of this chapter says "with senior citizens"—because we have been partners with seniors in California in our crime prevention efforts and this has been the secret of our success.

My office first became interested and concerned with senior's crime and consumer fraud problems in 1971 at about the time of the White House Conference on Aging where crime was one of several concerns that emerged. Research done by our staff at that time convinced us that crime prevention programs and legislation were greatly needed. Recent research in the spring of 1975 shows this still to be true. All reports on seniors indicate a greatly increasing fear of burglary and street crimes such as mugging and purse snatching. For example, although the recent Harris Poll commissioned by the National Council on Aging reveals that the general public perceives the elderly condition to be worse than the seniors report, still the largest number of seniors noted "fear of crime" ahead of all others as a "very serious" problem.

Our experience of three years working with seniors and our recent research in California reemphasizes the special vulnerability of the elderly to certain kinds of crime—burglary and street crime, buncos, medical quackery, and consumer frauds. Although in percentages seniors may not suffer proportionately as many major "crimes against person," as young males, for example, the results of criminal assault upon the elderly are more traumatic physically, financially, and psychologically.

The special vulnerability of senior citizens to criminal victimization results generally from physical deterioration attendant upon the process of aging and the economic factors resulting in severe financial deprivation for our elderly population so that the economic loss from crime against person or property has a considerably heavier impact upon the elderly than the rest of the population.

The increasing fear of crime among our elderly has become almost epidemic, and we must alleviate this fear by convincing them that they are not powerless to prevent victimization and that law enforcement is concerned and prepared to support and assist them.

Profile of California's Elderly

In California, seniors over 65 make up about 10 percent of our population, or approximately 2 million persons, and the prognosis is for increase—some projections indicate 20 percent by the year 2000. Approximately 30 percent of persons over 65 years live alone or with nonrelatives, and of those, 74 percent are women. Women constitute 59 percent of the senior population, and senior women are victimized by certain crimes—purse snatch, robbery, bunco schemes—in substantially greater proportion than other population categories.

In California, 41 percent of the senior citizens live in the central cities of our urbanized areas, and in these areas crimes of force and consumer frauds appear to have the heaviest impact upon the elderly. A typical profile of an elderly person in a major city finds him or her:

1. Living on social security, or a limited and fixed retirement income
2. Living in small quarters often in low-rent apartments or rooms in high crime areas
3. Isolated, lonely, and convinced of the necessity to barricade himself or herself at dusk out of fear of intruders
4. With increasing health and mobility problems
5. With limited transportation resources

Crimes of Force

The crimes of force to which California elderly are most vulnerable appear to be street crimes—particularly the purse snatch directed toward senior women—and burglary in certain urban areas. A statistical picture of the incidence of crimes of force upon the elderly in Los Angeles is revealed by a recent U.S. Census Bureau survey of crime. Of those surveyed who were over 65 years of age, 1 in 56 seniors had suffered a theft (burglary or auto theft); 1 in 73 had been assaulted; 1 in 188 was a victim of purse snatch; 1 in 204 was a victim of robbery; and 1 in 440 was a victim of attempted robbery.

In working with seniors, our crime prevention unit has developed methods of prevention to minimize the likelihood of victimization by these crimes. Detailed information on residential target hardening teaches inexpensive methods of improving resistance to forceful entry through windows and doors, the importance of thinning and lowering shrubbery for visual survey, and other methods of discouraging entry. We encourage self-help projects such as neighbor-hood watch, Operation I.D., organized security checks, and partnership with local law enforcement in these and other deterrent strategies.

With respect to purse snatch, there is simple instruction given on carrying money and credit cards in inside pockets of clothing instead of in a purse, methods of carrying purses for quick release to minimize physical injury, and avoidance factors related to place and time.

Concerning assault, seniors are trained in techniques of avoidance, including when and where to walk, carrying whistles or sirens for deterrence, and the use of the buddy system.

It is important when working with seniors in preventing crimes of force that emphasis be given to the positive aspect of prevention efforts in order to minimize the pervasive climate of fear. It has been noted that seniors often fear crimes of personal violence considerably out of proportion to the actual likelihood of incidence. We need to combat fear by the demonstration of law enforcement's concern and by presenting concrete evidence of successes in prevention programs involving both law enforcement and self-help and mutual aid efforts. It is image bolstering to seniors, for example, for law enforcement to recognize their special availability and usefulness for neighborhood or block watch strategies.

Bunco and Confidence Games

Although it is unfortunately true that California seniors are experiencing increased incidence and fear of crimes of force, the fact of the matter is that they are even more vulnerable to certain nonforce crimes. Crimes of a bunco and confidence nature are almost exclusively directed toward the senior citizen. The San Francisco and Los Angeles police departments report that more than 90 percent of the bunco victims are over 65 years of age and are mainly women. In California, the predominant bunco schemes victimizing our elderly are the "bank examiner" scheme; the "pigeon drop" scheme; and the welfare, social security, and pension check frauds. In one six-month period in the Los Angeles Police Department's jurisdiction, almost twice as much money was lost by seniors through the bank examiner and pigeon drop con games as was lost by banks through robberies. Recently, evidence is surfacing that our efforts and those of local law enforcement are resulting in diminution of bunco incidence. This evidence comes from participants in our crime prevention programs and from reports of the Division of Law Enforcement in the State Department of Justice. In the San Francisco Bay area, an intensive media campaign on bunco methods of operation was undertaken. In the period of January to June 1975, the San Francisco Police Department recorded 24 bank examiner attempts and only one loss ($4,000). Twenty-three recognized the scheme and foiled the attempt by calling the police.

The vulnerability of seniors to buncos and con games results from their isolation, their economic distress, and the fact that their life savings are usually readily accessible in bank or savings and loan accounts. Bunco prevention consists of teaching them to recognize the M.O.'s of the various bunco schemes and of frequent reinforcement of a few simple rules:

1. Never discuss your personal finances with strangers.
2. Don't expect to get something for nothing.
3. Never draw cash out of a bank or savings account at the suggestion of a stranger.
4. Always check on anyone who claims to be an FBI agent, bank official, official inspector, or representative of any public agency.
5. Do call the police and report any bunco M.O. approaches.

We also train personnel of California banking and saving institutions on bunco M.O.'s and victimization patterns, and enlist their cooperation in public education programs at their various branches.

In the effort to improve bunco prevention methodology for local law enforcement, our department's Division of Law Enforcement through the Crime Patterns Analysis section of the Organized Crime and Criminal Intelligence Branch, develops special investigative training materials and information-sharing procedures for local law enforcement personnel. Crime reporting by law enforcement relating to bunco schemes has not, in the past, been uniform. In an attempt to corrolate cases and identify problem areas, we are training law enforcement investigators throughout the state in the use of standard crime report forms for these schemes.

Medical Quackery

In California, quackery is estimated to be about a $50 million business. Common "get well quick" schemes include cures for cancer, arthritis, baldness, obesity, restoration of youthful vigor, and, yes, even the common cold! Economic loss is substantial and delay in receiving proper medical treatment while dealing with the quack may lead to more serious medical problems and even death.

A prime target of the medical quack is the senior citizen. Vulnerability arises out of the obvious fact that as the aging process unfolds, concomitant deterioration of physical condition and increase of health problems occur. Further, the more serious the health problem and the less susceptible to cure or amelioration by legitimate medical services, the more desperate the sufferer becomes and the more likely he or she is to resort to "miracle cures."

Indications are that seniors are the victims in approximately seven in every ten cases of medical quackery fraud coming to the attention of the criminal justice system. In addition to informing seniors of the details of specific current schemes, we instruct them in methods of identifying the medical quack including the following guidelines:

1. Any person who guarantees to be able to cure a disease is suspect.
2. Avoid the practitioner who has a secret formula or a special treatment known only to him.
3. Legitimate medical practitioners usually do not advertise their services.
4. Great success by quacks is achieved through direct mailing.
5. Some food fadism and false nutritional therapy are special types of quackery.

Emphasis is placed on checking the legitimacy and qualifications of anyone offering medical help and, in the case of such devices as hearing aids, checking whether a provider is appropriately licensed by the state.

Consumer Frauds: Crimes of the Marketplace

Our experience in California, in addition to our recent research in surveying district attorneys' consumer fraud units, the State Department of Consumer Affairs, local law enforcement, and local senior committees, indicates the particular consumer crimes to which seniors are the most subject. Additionally, it must be remembered that seniors suffer greatly from consumer fraud in general due to their condition of substantial economic deprivation. The loss of $5 in a consumer transaction has a financial impact upon seniors that is substantially greater than a similar loss by members of the working population.

In training seniors with respect to crimes in the marketplace, we take a two-fold approach—the first is to deal in depth with special areas of consumer crime and the second is to deal with general guidelines to the avoidance of consumer frauds common in the marketplace.

As to consumer crimes most frequently victimizing our elderly, one area of concern involves supplementary health insurance and medical plans. Because of their unique health problems, seniors are particularly vulnerable to the so-called "suede shoe" salespersons peddling these plans door-to-door. Prevention training includes: (1) refraining from impulse buying with respect to health plans; (2) recognizing that oral commitments have no validity unless included in a written contract; (3) consulting with public authorities as to the licensing and reputation of corporations selling health plans; and (4) consulting for translation of legal and small print terminology regarding benefits into understandable terms.

Seniors are also particularly victimized by mail order frauds. The mail order business is a hazardous area since post office boxes may be taken out under false names of businesses that do not, in fact, exist. One modus operandi of the mail order fraud operator is to insert ads in magazines and newspapers and give a post office box for return of monies. The media do not attempt to check the validity of such ads. The mail order con artists also operate through use of bulk mailings, using the telephone book and addressing their ads to "resident" or "occupant."

In connection with mail order frauds, we work closely with the United States postal inspector in the state and attempt to provide ongoing education on current victimization schemes. Schemes currently most common in California involve work-at-home offers, popular because seniors are desperately anxious to supplement their incomes. Perhaps the most common of such frauds involves offering work in addressing and stuffing envelopes. Seniors sending in their money to secure work may not in return receive work but simply get a sheet of instructions on how to search for such work. Other common mail order schemes include offers to make products in the home, franchise schemes such as the purchase of vending machines, pyramid sales, chain letter schemes, "estate searches," phony puzzle contests, and "free" offers.

Other areas of consumer crime to which seniors are vulnerable include auto repairs, home repairs, mobile homes, and door-to-door sales. We train the elderly in the provisions of the consumer law in general covering areas regarding contracts, retail installment buying and credit problems. We educate seniors to recognize various deceptive sales practices including bait and switch, deceptive pricing, fear-sell techniques, false descriptions of goods or services, referral selling, unordered merchandise, collection practices, and the law with respect to garnishment.

In consumer fraud education, we outline the role of the various public legal offices in the enforcement of California consumer law. It is important that seniors know that public law offices, whether state or local, cannot sue in behalf of one individual citizen who may have been defrauded in an effort to recover that individual's monetary loss but that they sue either criminally or civilly in behalf of all of the people of the state or local jurisdiction bringing legal action against alleged violators of the law. To assist individual seniors to seek redress of marketplace fraud, we detail all the resources available.

New Crime Prevention Training Program for
Aging Agency Personnel

In the year ahead, our crime prevention unit will undertake a new effort to "multiply the hands" and maximize the impact of expertise and methodology we have developed. We are entering into a partnership with the State Office on Aging, and the regional and local area agencies on aging to train those persons in daily contact with seniors. Agencies on aging will bring together both staff and volunteers who directly serve seniors for one-day workshop sessions where they will be trained both in subject matter and "how to" formats and will be provided with extensive written resource materials.

Our experience in California has demonstrated that segmental crime prevention efforts provide concrete results, proved the effectiveness of mobilizing interagency resources in the community, and validated the benefits of partnership between seniors and law enforcement.

One of the training tools we have developed is a bimonthly "Senior Crime Preventer's Bulletin" that alerts seniors to current crimes and schemes against them throughout California, presents in-depth education in the areas of crime to which they are susceptible and provides action models. The bulletin is received by all seniors who participate in our crime prevention seminars in local communities and is used as a training tool by law enforcement and senior citizen agencies of local governments. Local agencies frequently duplicate the training materials and regularly circulate them.

To ascertain the validity of this training program, all recipients of the bulletin were sent an evaluation questionnaire in the March-April 1975 issue. We received a 94 percent positive evaluation (total number of respondents represented 57 percent seniors and 43 percent law enforcement agencies) from all respondents. Significantly, the response from law enforcement agency personnel was 100 percent positive.

In response to uses to which the bulletin is put, 89 percent said they pass along the information to organizations, local officials, and so forth. The bulletin is reproduced in whole or in part by at least 50 publications in the state. Law enforcement indicate they use it in both recruit and in-service training, at roll call, in school presentations and in other programs. Those in the educational field indicate that teachers use the materials in consumer education, home economics, and business classes.

One of the questions was directed to eliciting examples of prevention projects undertaken as well as actual cases of avoided victimization. Response showed that there had been cases of concrete avoided victimization in bunco, mail order frauds, purse snatch, possible assault, door-to-door frauds, home repairs, and others. Among examples of crime prevention action undertaken by individuals and/or organizations were: group check cashing, utility bill paying, and grocery shopping activities; the institution of neighborhood coffee klatch discussions with local police invited; entire meetings devoted to in-depth discussion of subject areas; various methods of informing seniors on important alerts in places where seniors gather; organized residential burglary checks; and cooperative efforts to provide inexpensive installation of residential target hardening devices.

We have proved that by mobilizing in a concerted effort all the resources available in the community effective action without additional cost can be realized. Over the years, this program has developed into an outstanding example of interagency cooperation and there follows a listing of some of the agencies that have joined with us in implementing this program:

At the state level: California's Department of Consumer Affairs; State Office on Aging; Corporations Commissioner; Insurance Commissioner; Department of Health; Department of Housing and Community Development; Department of Real Estate; Department of Motor Vehicles; and the Franchise Tax Board, among others

At the federal level: Federal Trade Commission; Food & Drug Administration; Social Security Administration; Federal Bureau of Investigation; and the U.S. Postal Service Mail Fraud Unit

At the local level: Local law enforcement (police and sheriff's departments); district attorneys; city attorneys; city and county consumer affairs agencies (sealers of weights and measures); departments of parks and recreation; city and county senior citizen departments; health and social service departments; community colleges and adult schools; universities and state colleges; city and county local government structures; poverty programs including legal aid societies; and other human resource agencies

At the private organization level: National and local senior citizen organizations; associations of retired government, transportation and other workers; churches; Better Business Bureau; Goodwill Industries; ethnic groups; local service clubs; women's organizations; financial and business institutions; and, most important-ly, local senior citizen clubs and individuals

It has long been my conviction that law enforcement must direct its efforts in a major thrust to develop the field of crime prevention, and everything that has happened in recent years reinforces that conclusion. We have witnessed consistently escalating rates of crime and must confess in all honesty that reliance upon the traditional police approach of apprehension prosecution and incarceration have failed to stem the tide.

Evidence is increasing that a substantial proportion of crimes are never reported to police agencies. Of those crimes reported, a very low percentage result in apprehension of suspects; the proportion of eventual convictions of such suspects is still a smaller percentage; and, in spite of our continual efforts at rehabilitation in penal institutions, recidivism rates are still discouragingly high.

The conclusion seems inescapable that although we must vigorously con-tinue our efforts to improve the effectiveness of traditional approaches, we cannot rely upon such efforts. Even if we should become in the future more vastly successful in dealing after the fact with criminal offenders and were to reap the presumed consequent benefits of improved deterrence that could flow therefrom, the devastating impact upon the victim of crime still remains. This impact in terms of physical, psychological, and financial loss cannot be redressed through apprehension and punishment of offenders.

These facts are being increasingly recognized in law enforcement throughout California, and today our police agencies are devoting major effort to research, program development, and the commitment of resources to the prevention of crime before the fact.

After nearly four years of leadership, we see an increasing disposition among local law enforcement in California to undertake segmental crime prevention programs in their local jurisdictions toward the prevention of elderly victimization. It is our hope that the criminal justice system throughout the nation, especially local law enforcement and public legal offices, will recognize the special problems and needs of elderly citizens and undertake concerted strategies to respond to those needs.

Index

Index

Active vulnerability, defined, 93
Advocacy programs, in crime prevention, 116-118; and victim, 3-4
Aged. *See* Elderly
Age-integrated housing, advantages, 67; and crime, 70-71; and fear of crime, 71-73. *See also* Isolation
Age-segregated housing, advantages, 67; and crime, 70-71; and crime prevention, 72-73; and fear of crime, 71-73; versus age-integrated housing, 94, 153-156
Aging, as victimization, 77
Aging process, 21-22, 27-28; social view of, 77-78
Archer, Dan, 65
Architecture, and crime prevention, 154-155, 156. *See also* Housing
Automobile, impact on police patrol, 45

Baker, Russell, 10
Block, Richard L., 52
Boggs, Sarah L., 52
Brostoff, Phyllis Mensh, 127
Brown, Roberta, 127
Burglary, of elderly, 47-48, 92; house versus apartment, 44, 46(t), 47(t)
Butler, Robert, 127

Cassell, J., 26
Cloward, Richard, 157
Community patrol groups, problems, 65
Community solidarity, and crime prevention, 64-65, 135; and crime rate, 108; and fear of crime, 60-62; in high crime versus low crime area, 105-107. *See also* Neighborhood cohesion; Social control
Confidence games, 161-162; as cultural product, 16
Conklin, John E., 51, 52
Consumer fraud, 163-164; fear of, 57
Credit card system, for elderly, 116-117

Crime, compensation, 15, 84, 87; as cultural product, 31; against elderly, types, 33(t), 91-92; exposure to, 23, 25, 26; fear of, elderly, 24-28, 93, 104-109, 159-160, 161; of force, 160-161; and housing, 70-71; and income, 35-38, 51; insurance system against, 84; multiple victims, 40(t); and penal reform, 8-9; police attitudes to, 122-123; in public housing projects, 24-26; public opinion, 24; and race of victim, 38(t); reporting by public, 94-95, 108. *See also separate types of crime*; Fear of crime; Police
Crime prevention, 156, 160-167; and age-segregated housing, 72-73; and architecture, 154-155, 156; citizen volunteer groups and, 49-50; community role, 4, 45-47; and community solidarity, 45-47, 64-65, 135; isolation and, 108; model, 113-118; and police, 166-167; public concern and, 50; public policy, 109, 134-137; training program for aging agency personnel, 164-166; and victim behavior, 86. *See also* Community solidarity; Defensible space; Project Assist; Safe zones
Crime rate, community perception, 105-108; growth, 1. *See also* Victimization rate
Crime victim, compensation, 15, 84, 87; program model, 113-118; state aid, 115. *See also* Victim
Crime Victim Service Program, 112, 117
Criminal, knowledge of police, 45; use of isolation, 108; versus victim, 14-15, 41-44, 83-86, 93. *See also* Offender; Youth
Criminal justice system, and elderly, 14-15; neglect of victim in, 3, 86-87;

171

About the Contributors

Phyllis Mensh Brostoff, M.S.W., is a Lecturer at the School of Social Welfare, University of Wisconsin-Milwaukee. Ms. Brostoff was Director of Project Assist in Washington, D.C., in 1970-1971 and has written on the relationship among police, social work and the elderly.

John E. Conklin, Ph.D., is Assistant Professor of Sociology, Tufts University. Dr. Conklin was the principal investigator on a robbery research project at the Center for Criminal Justice at Harvard Law School in 1969-1970. Dr. Conklin is also author of *Robbery and the Criminal Justice System* (Lippincott, 1972) and *The Impact of Crime* (MacMillan, 1975).

Carl L. Cunningham, M.A., is Chief of Evaluation and Data Analyses, Office of Transportation Safety, Illinois Department of Transportation. Mr. Cunningham was Principal Social Scientist at Midwest Research Institute and is the author of numerous papers and articles on crime against the elderly and other criminal justice topics.

John P.J. Dussich,, Ph.D., is Coordinator, Research and Evaluation Unit, Bureau of Criminal Justice Planning and Assistance, State of Florida. Dr. Dussich has worked extensively in the area of victim advocacy and victim services. Dr. Dussich is also author of "The Victim Ombudsman: A Proposal" in Drapkin and Viano, *Victimology: A New Focus* (Lexington Books, 1974).

Charles J. Eichman, candidate in Philosophy, is Research Administrator, Institute for the Advanced Study of Correctional Effectiveness (Tallahassee, Florida). Mr. Eichman has published extensively in the area of corrections.

Steven Feldman, B.A., is a research associate at the Philadelphia Geriatric Center.

David M. Friedman, M.U.R.P., is Administrator, Mount Sinai Medical Center in New York City. Mr. Friedman was Associate Project Director of the Crime Victims Service Center, Bronx, New York in 1973-1975.

Gilbert Geis, Ph.D., is Professor, Program in Social Ecology, University of California, Irvine. Dr. Geis has served as a consultant to the President's Committee on Narcotic and Drug Abuse, the President's Commission on Law Enforcement and Administration of Justice, and the National Commission on Causes and Prevention of Violence. Dr. Geis has published extensively including *Public Compensation to Victims of Crime* (Praeger, 1974), *Man, Crime, and*

Society - 2nd ed. (Random House, 1970) and *White-Collar Criminal: The Offender* in Business and the Professions (Atherton, 1968).

M. Powell Lawton, Ph.D., is Director, Behavioral Research, Philadelphia Geriatric Center. Dr. Lawton is a Past President of the Division on Adult Development and Aging of the American Psychological Association. Dr. Lawton has published extensively in the gerontology field including *Planning and Managing Housing for the Elderly* (Wiley-Interscience, 1975).

James T. Mathieu, Ph.D., is Assistant Professor of Sociology, at Loyola-Marymount University in Los Angeles. Dr. Mathieu is a Fulbright Lecturer at the University of Zambia in Africa for 1975-1976.

Lucille Nahemow, Ph.D., is Senior Research Scientist, Philadelphia Geriatric Center and Adjunct Associate Professor of Psychology, New York University. Dr. Nahemow has done extensive environmental research about the elderly.

Anne D. Nelson, M.S.W., is a research assistant with Welfare Research, Inc., in Albany, New York.

Evelyn S. Newman, M.L.S., is project coordinator on a project on options in intermediate sheltered housing for the elderly at the School of Social Welfare of the State University of New York at Albany. Ms. Newman was the project coordinator for the Crime and Aged Study.

Jeffrey H. Reiman, Ph.D., is Associate Professor at the Center for the Administration of Justice, The American University. Dr. Reiman has published in the area of the philosophy of criminal justice including *In Defense of Political Philosophy* (Harper and Row, 1972) and *Police and Society* (D.C. Heath, 1975).

James B. Richardson, M.A., is a planner with the Office of Justice Programs, City of Portland, Oregon. Mr. Richardson was a crime analyst for the Portland Police Bureau and has published in the police field.

Edmund A. Sherman, Ph.D., is Associate Professor at the School of Social Welfare, State University of New York at Albany. Dr. Sherman was Project Director of the Crime and Aged Study at the Institute of Gerontology. Dr. Sherman has done several studies on the needs of the elderly.

Richard A. Sundeen, Ph.D., is Assistant Professor at the School of Public Administration, University of Southern California. Dr. Sundeen has published articles on diversion of juveniles and on fear of crime among the elderly.

Richard E. Sykes, Ph.D., is Senior Staff Research Advisor at Minnesota Systems Research, Inc. and Assistant Professor of Sociology, University of Minnesota. Dr. Sykes has published a number of articles on police-community relations and police organization.

David P. Van Buren, M.A., is a Security Coordinator for the Albany Housing Authority, Albany, New York. Mr. Van Buren is a Ph.D. candidate at the School of Criminal Justice, State University of New York at Albany and was a research assistant on the Crime and Aged Study.

Emilio C. Viano, Ph.D., is Associate Professor at the Center for the Administration of Justice, The American University. Dr. Viano is the author of several articles, is coauthor of *Social Problems and Criminal Justice* (Nelson-Hall, 1975) and is coeditor of *Victimology* (Lexington Books, 1974), *Victimology: A New Focus* (Lexington Books, 1975) and *Police and Society* (Lexington Books, 1975). Dr. Viano is also Editor-in-Chief of *Victimology: An International Journal.*

Silvia Yaffe, M.A., is a research associate at the Philadelphia Geriatric Center. Ms. Yaffe has published a number of articles in gerontology.

Evelle J. Younger, LL.B., is Attorney General of the State of California. Attorney General Younger has also served as a judge on both the Los Angeles Superior Court and Los Angeles Municipal Court as well as Deputy Los Angeles City Attorney and Pasadena City Prosecutor. He has published many legal articles and is responsible for the founding of the California Department of Justice's Consumer Information and Protection Program for Seniors.

About the Editors

Jack Goldsmith, Ph.D., is Associate Professor at the Center for the Administration of Justice and Director of the Institute for Law Enforcement Management at The American University. Dr. Goldsmith was the Chairman of the National Conference on Crime Against the Elderly and has written extensively in the area of crime and the elderly. Dr. Goldsmith edited a "Symposium on Crime Against the Elderly" in *The Police Chief* (February, 1976) and coedited *The Police Community: Dimensions of an Occupational Subculture* (Palisades Publishers, 1974).

Sharon S. Goldsmith, M.A., is Lecturer at the Center for the Administration of Justice, The American University. Ms. Goldsmith was the Program Coordinator for the National Conference on Crime Against the Elderly and has testified before the Federal Council on Aging on "Crime and the Older Woman." Ms. Goldsmith has written papers and articles on crime and the elderly and is coeditor of *The Police Community: Dimensions of an Occupational Subculture* (Palisades Publishers, 1974).